Queens' SECRETS

Queens' Secrets
Copyright © 2021 Yasmin Teimoori
First published in 2021

Print: 978-1-922456-71-7
E-book: 978-1-922456-72-4
Hardback: 978-1-922456-70-0

All rights reserved. No part of this book may be reproduced, stored in a retrieval system, or transmitted by any means (electronic, mechanical, photocopying, recording, or otherwise) without written permission from the author.

Because of the dynamic nature of the Internet, any web addresses or links contained in this book may have changed since publication and may no longer be valid. The information in this book is based on the author's experiences and opinions. The views expressed in this book are solely those of the author and do not necessarily reflect the views of the publisher; the publisher hereby disclaims any responsibility for them.

The author of this book does not dispense any form of medical, legal, financial, or technical advice either directly or indirectly. The intent of the author is solely to provide information of a general nature to help you in your quest for personal development and growth. In the event you use any of the information in this book, the author and the publisher assume no responsibility for your actions. If any form of expert assistance is required, the services of a competent professional should be sought.

Publishing information
Publishing, design, and production facilitated by Passionpreneur Publishing,
A division of Passionpreneur Organization Pty Ltd
ABN: 48640637529

www.PassionpreneurPublishing.com
Melbourne, VIC | Australia

Queens' SECRETS

Timeless Beauty Rituals Inspired By Nature, Made In The Kitchen

Yasmin Teimoori

Contents

01 ANCIENT BEAUTY CARE HABITS

Ancient Beauty Care Habits / 5

02 ESSENTIAL OILS

Benefits of Essential Oils / 15
5 Ways of Using Essential Oils in Our Beauty Routine / 15
Ageless Beauty and Massage / 17
Safety guidelines and general precautions to use Essential oils / 18
Common Essential Oils / 18
Carrier Oils & Why Are They Needed? / 26
Top 5 Picks for Carrier Oils to Have At Home / 27
The Concept of Synergy Blends / 29

03 NUMINOUS CHINA

Goodbye Blackheads & Open Pores Mask / 37
Ginger Honey Mask / 37
Ginseng & Green Tea Mask / 38
Chinese Empress Pearl Mask / 39
Chinese Green Papaya Mask / 40
Mung Bean Face Mask for Acne / 41
Anti-Ageing Mung bean Face Mask / 42
Glowing Skin with Almond / 42
Ancient Chinese Empress Herbal Bath / 43

04 REGAL INDIA

Sacred Neem in Indian Beauty Routine / 47
Neem Hair Mask / 48
Indian Whitening Exfoliation Mask / 48
Mango Mousse Cream / 49
Acne Scars Treatment / 50
Multani Mitti in Indian Beauty Care / 51
AMLA, Perfect hair's secret / 53

05 ALLURING KOREA

JUDO Cleansing and Whitening Scrub / 60
Korean Brightening Face Mask / 61
Prank up Acne Mask / 62
Mermaid Face Mask / 63
Korean Inspired Rice Cream / 64
Myeonyak Facial Medicine / 65

06 MYSTERIOUS EGYPT

Queen Nefertari Beauty Secrets / 71
Queen Cleopatra's Beauty Recipes / 74
Cleopatra's Bath / 74
Cleopatra's Cream / 75

07 GRAND PERSIA

Sidr & Yogurt Hair Mask / 82
How To Make Sormeh / 83
Saffron & Sandalwood Face Mask / 84
Saffron Face Pack For Dull Skin / 85
Potato Starch Masks to lighten the skin colour / 87
Pomegranate & Papaya Face Pack For Glowing Skin / 88

CHAPTER 01

ANCIENT BEAUTY CARE HABITS

CHAPTER 01
ANCIENT BEAUTY CARE HABITS

ANCIENT BEAUTY CARE HABITS

In ancient times we find narrations that are driven by women's striking beauty spurring men to murder, causing wars, influenced Art, and bringing artists and poets to ink down praises and supplications on them. It was their beauty that instigated wars like the Trojan War and toppled the thrones. Beauty has been a significant factor for women to find suitable partners. It was in those times when a women's worth was weighed or decided according to her attractiveness and allure.

I have traveled throughout the world since the age of 20 years and explored different lands, countries, and cultures rich in beauty and exquisiteness. My keen interest in the beauty and the rituals to maintain had gained momentum when I learned that every country has explicit traditional practices to preserve and enhance their beauty.

Women in every century have been particular and conscious about appearing beautiful and embellishing the world with their attractiveness. There are abundant of natural remedies that women around the globe included in their daily life to enhance and treat their skin. My curiosity gave birth to an urge to discover and compile skin rituals, ingredients, and practices that have benefitted women for centuries. These natural beauty augmenting recipes vary from South Asia countries to Russia and many others on the map.

In today's world, cosmetic surgeries have become a trending fashion, and women find satisfaction in chemicals drugs to beautify their bodies. However, natural remedies and elements are deep-rooted in every society and are practiced widely in every society. Women resonate well with nature to bring out and boost their charm and attraction. Their devotion and assurance in natural products are unmatchable. The advances and scientific progress in beauty care and formulas have enticed women towards them but were not magnetic enough to pull them away from the natural ingredients doing wonders for their skin and body.

I do not oppose the idea of cosmetic surgeries. It is one of the greatest human achievements which has turned around the world of fashion and beauty. Cosmetic surgery's basic function is to improve and enhance one's appearance. It leaves me in awe to think that now people can improve their features and get rid of skin issues which seemed impossible to cure in past centuries. It gives us enough area to align our natural features with our desired structure of a specific body part e.g. nose, lips, liposuction, etc. It further improves physical health such as respiratory issues are subsided after nose Rhinoplasty. This advancement of cosmetic surgery does not only improve the looks of people but it boosts their confidence and self-esteem. It makes people accept themselves more than before. For a happy life, it is important to love yourself and Cosmetic surgery plays a huge role in it. It gives you an opportunity to enhance your beauty and feels confident about yourself. Insecurities that are engraved in your mind are also eliminated with the change brought in your feature.

However, unnecessarily getting yourself treated to conform to the trending fashion is the abuse of this advancement. A step taken to enhance any feature should be wisely thought. Undergoing the knife excessively may cause harm instead of beautifying your natural features. It is better to treat and look after yourself before taking drastic features and as it is said prevention is better than cure.

One thing that I realized was that apart from women enjoying these natural remedies, many five-star spas and salons worldwide had opted for these and included them as their special service due to their potency and ancient value. Several ancient royal treatments were an essential part of the royal ladies' routine. The spas celebrated the old reliable ingredients and treated their client's skin-related concerns with these treatments.

I had the opportunity of working and owning a spa in UAE since 2001. My spa had professionals hired from all around the world. Why did I hire people from every country rich in beauty care? My motive was to give the best natural beauty care treatments to clients from all cultures under one roof.

Beauty would seem to be a fundamental experience of human beings in any society, ancient or modern. Can there be a culture that has no such concept, or no term to express it?

The beauty of a woman as in common is related to skin and hair unanimously. The beautiful skin and hair of a person give a perceptual experience of satisfaction. But have you ever thought that how you can have a glowing skin and volumized manageable hair and keep it for the rest of your life?

Going through the history of ancient civilised societies, I have learned about some other factors that have been believed to have a direct influence on physical attractiveness

---

Ayurveda is an ancient medical science which was developed in India. Ayurveda deals with all the aspects of human life. Since an early age, human life has a great impact on the external appearance of oneself. Skin is the basic element of external appearance. Beauty is generally dependent on the type and texture of the skin one has. Also, the beauty is not only dependent on the skin but also on other factors like hair falling, hair blackening,

- Roopam is outer beauty — personified by shining, healthy hair and a clear, radiant complexion.
- Gunam refers to inner beauty — the beauty that shines from within, characterized by a warm, pleasing personality and innocence of mind and heart.
- And vayastyag means lasting beauty — looking, and feeling, younger than your chronological age. Thus, Ayurveda does not focus only on cosmetics to achieve a state of true beauty.

Roopam does not specify a type of figure or the color of the skin or the length or style of the hair. Outer beauty, according to Ayurveda, is a reflection of good health — good digestion and healthy eating habits and lifestyle. The frame of the body is dependent on the type of structural components you were born with. Whether thin, medium, or big, each type of body structure can be beautiful as long as good health exists.

You are what you eat. Ayurveda takes this notion very seriously. In fact, it goes a step further to say "You are what you digest." A radiant, clear complexion begins with proper nutrition, efficient digestion and assimilation of nutrients by the body, and regular elimination. It's all about

diet. There are simple ayurvedic principles you can follow, even if you are a newcomer to the system.

Gunam is the attribute of Mind and Spirit. A beautiful mind is well balanced in the TRI GUNAS- Sattva- Rajas - Tamas. The three gunas are the most subtle qualities of Nature that underlie matter, life, and mind. They are the energies through which not only the surface mind but our deeper consciousness functions. Gunam reflects the beauty of our mind and soul and manifests itself as thoughts, actions, and words. Our Gunam is governed by three main mental functions; learning, retaining, and long-term memory and recall. A well-disciplined mind that is coordinated with our senses and inner consciousness will indeed behave beautifully.

And finally, Vayastyag, the everlasting beauty is focused on how we can look younger than our chronological age and is supported by both roopam and gunam beauty. Vayastyag in itself is a complete science of how to achieve lasting beauty through shri kamya rasayanas or skin rejuvenating regimes to slow down the aging process and promote luster and beauty. Premature Ageing in Ayurveda is caused due to an imbalance in doshas, dhatus, and Agni, due to an erratic diet and lifestyle. This everlasting beauty can be maintained through diet- lifestyle- medicines, and therapies, to bring a balance in the levels of Doshas Dhatus Malas and Agni to achieve optimum health.

In ancient Persia as well, people believed that the face was a reflection of the soul. So, inner peace, great manner, and sinless soul will lead to having a beautiful and attractive face while negative emotions like jealousy, unfaithfulness and etc would lead to have an aging and wrinkled skin.

The book of Esther in the Old Testament describes what's going on in Persia at the time, Esther was put into the position of the queen because of her outer beauty, but she found favour with the king because of her inner beauty. She was given prominence and King Xerxes respected her which is why he would listen to her and ignore all the other women in his harem.

On the other side of the world, Ancient Greeks believed that one's physical, outward appearance was a reflection of one's inner character. If one was outwardly beautiful, one must also be inwardly pure and virtuous. The body was of utmost importance, and the physical was strongly linked to the moral in Greek minds and culture.

Nowadays, we all know that it's not just a bright smile that makes us shine when we are feeling good, positive emotions like happiness and joy release Endorphins and Neurotransmitters that reduce inflammation in the skin and will increase blood flow to the face which results in what others see as glow in our skin.

In a busy world with stressful lifestyles, it is essential to take time out for a little stillness and mindfulness self-care. High-stress levels, worries, and negative emotions not only cause serious health issues but also wrinkling laxity, and aging of the skin. Your skin is an essential part of your body, the same as your lungs and heart. The skin is the covering of your body, and if no care is taken of the cover than other organs can be affected. It is one of the barriers to infection and germs. Having a cracked skin untreated can leave you with an unattractive appearance and prone to infections. Therefore, healthy skin is not only the symbol of beauty but of wellbeing too.

Beauty is an amalgamation of a healthy body and mind. You cannot achieve everlasting beauty if anyone of these thing remains missing. Everything requires a delicate balance. The heart needs to be purified, the mind requires peace, and the skin needs care. With all these together you would gain an unmatched beauty which will remain forever. Your inner beauty reflects your outer beauty. To make your outward pretty along with skincare regimes, peace, positivity, and love are required. These are the main ingredients for the recipe of eternal beauty. Emotional wellness is linked to hormonal balance which is responsible for a calm mind and beauty.

What makes emotional wellbeing a necessity for your skin, hair, and beauty?

There are days when stress and tensions take over. Have you noticed that during those days usually your skin starts to break out and pimples occur on your skin? This happens not because you are not taking care of your skin; instead, it is the result of different hormonal changes caused due to stress in your body. The skin is directly affected by the emotional dilemma your body is facing. Moreover, your beauty affects your mental health and self-esteem, as well. Extreme hair fall, breakouts, and other skin issues hurt your self-esteem. It shatters your confidence and makes you feel less accepted around people. Clear, glowing skin and hair boosts your confidence, increases self-assurance and self-esteem. To keep your beauty and attraction intact, one must follow an effective skincare regime.

My experiences around the world have broadened my horizon, and I have come to a conclusion that every era, civilization, and place have in one way or the other prioritized skincare and beauty. Both men and women put in efforts to improve their skin, hair, and appear beautiful. Your beauty complements your personality and helps you to be one of the most appealing people in your gathering. Redefining natural beauty requires the right products, guidance, consistency, and efforts. Beauty regimes, when followed religiously change your skin from dull, dead, and uneven to glowing, radiant, and rejuvenated. Your beauty requires your attention. With the right amount of attention, your beauty will outshine you among the crowd.

CHAPTER 02
ESSENTIAL OILS

Benefits of Essential Oils/ 15
5 Ways of Using Essential Oils in Our Beauty Routine/ 15
Ageless Beauty and Massage/ 17
Safety guidelines and general precautions to use Essential oils/ 18
Common Essential Oils/ 18
Carrier Oils & Why Are They Needed?/ 26
Top 5 Picks for Carrier Oils to Have At Home/ 27
The Concept of Synergy Blends/ 29

CHAPTER 02
ESSENTIAL OILS

The world has been benefitting from the presence, properties, and qualities of Essential oil since centuries. You might wonder that these are famous in your times; however, it will come as a surprise that in every age Essential oils were religiously being used for various purposes throughout history. The earliest trace of Essential Oils can be found in the oldest civilisations, including Roman, Greek, Chinese, and Indian Ayurveda.

Ancient Egypt can be considered as the true birthplace of Essential oils or commonly known as Aromatherapy. The Egyptian beauty icon, Cleopatra, is said to have known the importance of incense and aromatic oils and used it accordingly. Moreover, these Oils were revered to the extent that only the priests were to use them as they were known to be one with the gods. Egyptians explored botany and extracted a wide range of these which were used in cosmetics and for religious and medicinal purposes. The interest and research of Egyptians were transferred to the Greeks who followed in the footsteps of Egyptians.

Hippocrates (c.460-377 BC), a renowned physician of that time, treated his patients holistically and realised the power of massage and Essential Oil being its major ingredient.

The healing and soothing properties of these oils left people in an excessive desire for them. China and India didn't lag in their research of herbs and aromatic plants. In ancient China, the great Yellow Emperor's, Huang Ti, book The Yellow Emperor's Book of Internal Medicine, mentions and discusses essential oils and is used as a basic guide for eastern medicine. Indian Ayurveda dates back to 3,000-year is overwhelmed with the use of Essential Oils.

In Roman times people were actively taking aromatic baths to keep their health intact. Skin burns and war injuries were widely treated with Essential oil concoctions. The burn marks often used to leave the skin unattractive and unpleasant were smoothed exceptionally well by their application. Essential Oils are natural ingredients that are being used for enhancing and beautifying our skin, body, and soul since eras.

Pedanius Dioscorides, a Greek physician, described in his five volumes of De Materia Medica, written between 50 and 70 CE, the healing powers of essential oils and the beliefs of that time. Later in the eleventh century, Avicenna isolated the essential compounds from plants using the distillation method, and since then, they have been widely used in medicine.

In 1910, French chemist and perfumer Rene Maurice Gattefosse burnt his hand in the laboratory and treated it immediately with undiluted lavender oil. The instant ease in pain and no hints of scars and infection made him realise the healing powers of Essential Oils.

In many pagan cultures and religions, these oils were used not only in religious practices and ceremonies but also for personal hygiene, Aromatherapy, and spiritual purposes. These oils have recently been revived by the cosmetic industry giants and have been in demand ever since. This has also given rise to the demand for alternative medicine which claims to cure certain medical conditions by the use of Aromatherapy.

Essential Oils also are known as volatile oils, ethereal oils, aetherolea, (Latin origin, refers to the distinct aromatic substance obtained from some plants), or only as of the oil of the plant from which they were extracted, such as oil of lavender. These are the essence of plants that are concentrated hydrophobic highly potent chemical compounds at times extremely volatile in nature, found in bark, flowers, seeds, and roots. The different properties, aromas, and scents have made them a popular ingredient in perfumes and beauty products. These are highly anti-microbial, anti-inflammatory, and anti-bacterial, and anti-oxidative properties enrich medicinal and cosmetic products. The interaction of the human body with Essential oils generates heeling, relaxing, soothing, and rejuvenating processes. Essential oils are mostly used in diluted forms as natural chemicals are raw and can sometimes cause irritation. The synergy blends- blends of different oils producing the same effect- are used to generate powerful and effective results when combined together. The different potions and mixtures can be used for particular skin problems and enhancement of your beauty and skin's health. People tend to mishear their skin's voice calling out for the necessary nutrients and vitamins required for its health. Essential oils can be included in your daily skincare routine to augment your skin's strength, health, and elasticity. These are essential to keep your skin youthful and glowing.

BENEFITS OF ESSENTIAL OILS

Essential oils have various benefits that one can enjoy. I have personally experienced these with every use of different Essential oils. Aromatherapy shows us that Essential oils are stress releasers and mood boosters. They have properties that not only benefit the body but the health of your mind as well. They are known for improving your night's sleep which is essential for your body's growth and proper functioning as many hormones become active to play their role. According to some studies, it is concluded that Essential oils improve immunity and reduce pain. They act as a catalyst for improved energy and mental clarity. Inflammatory conditions are also alleviated by using oil with the right properties. Many of the Essential Oils have antibacterial, antifungal, and antimicrobial properties that fight bacterial, fungal, and microbial diseases. The conditions of such diseases have improved drastically with the use of these oils. To sum it up, Essential oils have been a part of herbal medicines and therapeutic treatments due to their healing powers and beneficial properties. They can be used as a natural healer to keep your emotional, physical, and mental health in good condition.

5 WAYS OF USING ESSENTIAL OILS IN OUR BEAUTY ROUTINE

Inhalation

The easiest way to allow the essential oil in your bloodstream is inhalation. As beginner users always need to make sure that how your body reacts and absorbs it. For a small test bring the chosen essential oil close to your nose and sniff it a bit.

Be careful, to not sniff it strongly as there is a possibility to inhale the micro-particles around the bottle.

If you do not want to adopt the direct inhaling method then the indirect inhaling option is the one for you. It reduces the chances of inhaling the particles and you can enjoy the aroma of it.

Apply the Essential Oil on a piece of cotton or cotton balls, a small piece of bed sheet, or cloth to let the Oil keep your mood elevated.

Diffusion

Through diffusion, the Essential Oils are evaporated in the air with the help of the use of a diffusion device. Diffusion spreads the particles in the air and removes the unwanted odor from the room. This will improve your sleep and reduces stress.

There are 4 main types of essential oil diffusers on the market today:

• Nebulizing Diffusers: It works by breaking down essential oils with force. It does not require any heat or water, therefore releasing the most concentrated and purest form of essential oil into the air, making it the best option for aromatherapy.

• Ultrasonic or Humidifying Diffusers: This type of diffuser uses kinetic or vibration to breakdown the essential oil into micro-particles, and disperse them into the air as anionic particles.

• Evaporative or Reed Diffusers: Similar to heat diffusers, this type of diffuser also distributes the oils via evaporation but using a fan instead.

• Heat Diffusers or Oil Burner: This type of diffuser heats the essential up until it evaporates into the air.

Tropical

Tropical application means the direct application of Essential Oils on the skin and massage treatment. Warning: It is important to note that even the mildest of oils like Lavender oil needs dilution of oil is necessary before applying it directly to the skin. Usually, we dilute the essential oil with a carrier oil such as Jojoba to a concentration, not more than 3-5%. A safe way to create a 3% concentrated essential oil is to use one teaspoon of carrier oil with 3 drops of essential oil. If you're still reluctant to use essential oils onto your skin, you can consider using them on your feet to test, since the skin is thick and less sensitive, and are far away from mucous membranes.

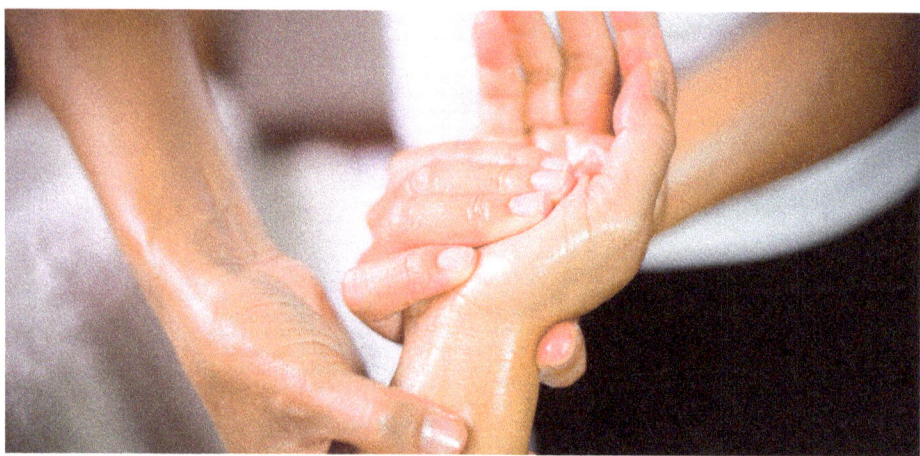

Bath

Before starting your aromatherapy bath, you must not add essential directly into your bath. Oil is hydrophobic, it doesn't mix with water at all. If you add essential oil directly into your bath and just hop into the bathtub, the highly concentrated oil has direct contact with your skin, and you might end up with a long-term sensitization with the oil. The only way to achieve this is to first mix essential oils with carrier oils like Jojoba or Coconut oil, then mix them into your bath. The optimal concentration is to add 3 to 12 drops of essential oil into one tablespoon of carrier oil. This concentration is relatively higher than the concentration you use topically, but not to worry because the entire tub of water will further dilute it for you. Aromatherapy baths can boost your mood, relieve your stress after a long working day, keep you relaxed throughout the day, cures headache, increase focus, get rid of allergy, and many

Diy Beauty Recipes

One fabulous way to use essential oils is with homemade creams, scrubs, soaps, lotions, and other lovely beauty products. What I love about DIY'ing skincare products at home is that you're listening to your body and mind to adapt, create, evolution, and/or reinforce the body, the mind, and the home environment. You're taking your power back essentially and saying 'I got this from mother earth!" It's an incredibly empowering experience. Every new season whether it's fall, winter, summer, or spring, I make 1-2 new recipes. My body and my mood always guide me in this way. To make things easy for you I've shared some of my top recipes in this book. As you become a DIY queen, you'll require to learn about essential oils for all your recipe needs.

AGELESS BEAUTY AND MASSAGE

Massage has been a part of beauty rituals from ancient times. It is known that massage can relieve your pain, reduce stress, and relax body muscles. Your exhausting routine can tire your body and drag it to the point of dullness and lifelessness. Massage strokes and movements remove the toxins from your body and relax your sore and fatigued muscles. It repairs your damaged tissues and improves blood circulation. It further loosens the muscle and eliminates the physical imbalances due to excessive work or improper posture. All these when treated together through massage become the reason for your ageless beauty. Your skin replenishes and rejuvenates with continuous massage and beauty is redefined. Also, emotional and mental health is made better with aromatic Essential Oils and massages which improves a person's overall health and beauty. If a person is physically and emotionally in good health it will reflect on their body and skin.

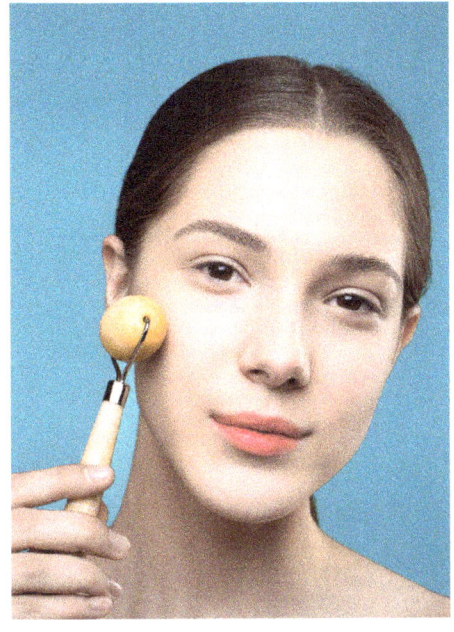

SAFETY GUIDELINES AND GENERAL PRECAUTIONS TO USE ESSENTIAL OILS

As many benefits, the Essential Oils carries it needs to be used with precautions because of the potential risk attached to it. Many of us are unaware of the risks which makes them hazardous if used in disproportionate quantity or combination. There are a few safety measures to be taken and considered before using the Essential Oils.

- Ensure the quality of the oil being used.
- Avoid contact with the eyes or mucus membranes.
- Ingestion of these should be done under the supervision of a professional therapeutic as they are highly concentrated and can damage the delicate lining of your stomach.
- People who suffer from ailments like epilepsy, high blood pressure, diabetes, and pregnant women and children should consider the methods and precautions before using it.
- Except for a few exceptional oils, others should not be used directly on the skin without being diluted.
- Some oils can be skin irritants and can cause dermatitis, burns. Therefore, a patch test should be done.
- Essential oils are volatile and therefore, should be stored in a dry and cold place.

COMMON ESSENTIAL OILS

Basil Oil

Basil Oil is being used since its discovery to benefit from the various properties that it holds within itself. This oil by sending messages to the brain improves and controls emotions of a person. There have been various researches which highlight that the use of basil oil aids in treating fungal, cancerous, and inflammatory issues. Basil oil's impressive presence of vitamin C, antiseptic and anti-inflammatory properties has made it popular for curing skin problems. Some of its benefits are:

- Ward offs skin irritation and sores
- Heals Eczema
- Improves skin cells metabolism and elasticity
- Unclogs pores
- Reduces acne and inflammation
- Cures diseases like ringworm infections.
- Anti-ageing properties reduce wrinkles.
- Improves complexion.
- Treats dandruff.

Bergamot Oil

Bergamot Essential Oil has a light citrusy smell. Its noticeable properties are antiseptic, antispasmodic, and analgesic (pain-relieving). The benefits for skin it carries are:

- Cures Acne
- Effective against painful cysts and pimples.
- Treats Eczema, ringworm infection, and psoriasis.

Chamomile Oil

Chamomile Essential Oil is used worldwide for ages for almost everything that can cross your mind. It is highly antispasmodic, antiseptic, antibiotic, antidepressant, tonic, bactericidal, sudorific, anti-inflammatory, and anti-infectious. It is used for the following purposes:
- Used for wound healing, including ulcers and sores.
- Easing skin conditions like Eczema or rashes.
- Subsides skin irritation and allergies.
- Detoxes skin.

Citronella Oil

Citronella Essential Oil is extracted from an Asian grass called Cymbopogon genus. This fragrant grass's name comes from the French word meaning "lemon balm," due to its floral, citrus-like aroma. It's used widely as an insect repellent. It's used for the following causes:
- As an insect repellent.
- As an antifungal agent.
- To treat parasitic infections.
- To promote wound healing.

Carrot Seed Oil

This oil may sound unfamiliar to most of you but has numerous advantages. Sometimes it is confused with carrot oil but of these have different properties. It is extracted from the seed of the Daucus carota plant that is used primarily for aromatherapy. The earthly and warm aroma of this oil soothes your mind and leaves you longing for it. The benefits it carries are:
- Anti-microbial
- Anti-oxidant
- Anti-inflammatory
- Anti-aging
- Stress and anxiety reliever

Cedar oil

Cedar wood is derived from the needles, leaves, bark, and berries of cedar trees. Cedar essential oil has potential health and beauty benefits that have been improving the health and skin of those who use it as a part of their routine. This essential oil is widely used as an insect repellent. Further, it improves your health by improving cerebral activity , increases concentration, decreases hyperactivity, osteoarthritis, cold, and cough, reduces harmful stress, eases tension, and enhances the quality of sleep. Below are some of the cosmetic issues that it can treat:

- Soothes irritation and inflammation
- Eliminates bacteria causing acne
- Eliminates unpleasant odors
- Reduces breakouts
- Protects skin from pollution.
- Improves overall skin health.
- Treats Eczema

Cinnamon Oil

Cinnamon Essential oil is one of the most celebrated essential oil in the cosmetic and medical world. This oil is extracted from the bark or leaves of several types of trees, including the Cinnamomum verum tree and the Cinnamomum cassia tree. The cinnamon oil properties make it popular for aromatherapy, medical and cosmetic purposes. Its properties are beneficial from boosting the immune system, metabolism, to improving respiration. The coagulant properties help to stem the flow of blood from cuts and assist the healing process. It also prevents cold, and aids in subsiding gastric issues. In cosmetics, it is reputed to calm and treat various issues. Some of them are given below:

- Alleviates dryness
- Slows the aging
- Address acne
- Cures rashes and infections
- Enhance circulation
- Nourish the skin
- Revives the skin tone

Clove Oil

The source of Clove Essential Oil is the Clove tree. It has a strong spicy aroma and its variety of applications has been benefitting in various fields. Its usage helps in respiratory and digestive uneasiness. Its anti- microbial properties make it effective in improving and healing your skin. Your skin becomes radiant and youthful by addressing the following with clove oil:
- Reduces sagginess of skin
- Prevents wrinkles and fine lines
- Slows down the aging process
- Removes dead cell
- Improves blood circulation

Eucalyptus Oil

Eucalyptus Essential Oil is one of the most celebrated oils throughout the world for its medicinal properties. The main ingredient is cineole (also known as eucalyptol), which is known for its anti-inflammatory, analgesic, and aromatic properties. It is considered a natural remedy for cold, cough, wounds, infections, and aches. Mind clarity is also achieved by the application of this valuable oil. In the cosmetic and beauty world its properties give you the following results:
- Treats minor burns
- Addresses injury
- Fights inflammation
- Promotes healing

Frankincense Oil

Frankincense Essential Oil, a natural astringent, is highly esteemed by ancient practitioners. It is, till the current date, used to alleviate the skin's health and spiritual connectedness. This oil has an earthy and uplifting aroma which makes it pleasurable to use. Some of its beauty benefits are:
- Soothes inflammation.
- Fades scars.
- Fights premature aging.
- Controlling acne.
- Anti-aging.
- Regulates sebum and controls oil.
- Stimulates cell regeneration.

Geranium Oil

Geranium Essential Oil has a sweet floral smell which makes it a suitable ingredient to be used in soaps, creams, and cosmetics. This oil plays an active role in improving the health of skin cells and enhancing the complexion. Its regular use results in:
- Regeneration of newer, healthier skin.
- Benefitting acne-prone skin
- Tightens the skin
- Diminishes the appearance of aging.
- Reduces sagging and wrinkling skin.
- Promote hair growth by nourishing the scalp
- Balances the production of sebum and natural oils.

Grape Oil

Grapefruit essential oil is a type of essential oil commonly used in aromatherapy. Sourced from the peel of the Citrus paradisi fruit. They are carriers of distinctive properties and aid in the betterment of the overall health and skin of a person. In the health domain, it assists in weight reduction, improves mood by curbing anxiety and stress, and lowers blood pressure. For skin, its antibacterial and antioxidant properties help in the treatment of acne. It also improves:

- Concentration
- Overall body health
- Increases vitality
- Uplifts moods.

Helichrysum Oil

Helichrysum Oil is recognized in Pharmacology because of the anti-inflammatory, antifungal, and antibacterial properties it carries. Helichrysum essential oil comes from the Helichrysum italicum plant commonly known as the curry plant. It has a strong curry-like smell, generally found in the Mediterranean and southern Europe. The oil can be extracted

from all green parts of the plant, including stems and leaves. A snippet of its benefits is given below:

- Helps to fight colds and coughs.
- Treats skin inflammation.
- Wipes out microbes that harm the skin.
- Fade blemishes.
- Heals wounds.
- Reduce muscle and joint inflammation

Jasmine Oil

The source of this oil is Jasmine flowering plant found in abundance in South Asia. Its charm lies in the gorgeous flowers having a sweet romantic fragrance which gives an aphrodisiac effect. It is a common product to treat health issues ranging from depression to infections. Some of the notable health benefits of this oil are the following:

- Prevents and treats oral infections
- Treats spasms
- Promotes wound healing
- Acts as an emollient
- Produces collagen
- Slows the aging period
- Comfort irritated, itchy, and dry skin
- Promotes sleep
- Evens skin tone
- Reduces dandruff and scalp irritation

Lavender Oil

It is one of the most cherished oil due to its herbal properties and floral aroma. This oil is used to treat issues varying from depression to insomnia. Other than these, for centuries, it has become a staple for skin cosmetics and medicines. This oil has anti-bacterial and anti-inflammatory properties. Its use improves the skin's health in the following manner:
- Reduces acne.
- Soothes Eczema and dry skin conditions.
- Reduce redness, blotchy patches, and acne scarring.
- Detoxifies skin.
- Heals injured skin and wounds.
- Prevents wrinkles.

Lemongrass Oil

Lemongrass essential oil is distilled from the leaves and woody stalks of the lemongrass plant. It is mostly found in countries with a tropical climate. Lemongrass oil is typically used to treat:
- Acne
- Anxiety
- Athlete's foot
- Excessive sweating
- Headaches
- Indigestion
- Muscle aches

Lemon oil

Lemon essential oil serves as a home health remedy. Extracted from the peels of fresh lemon this oil is effective in fighting exhaustion, depression, clears skin, pain reliever, and kills harmful bacteria and viruses. Antimicrobial, antifungal, astringent helps in improving your skins healthy in the following ways:
- Prevents skin inflammation
- Reduces skin irritation
- Enhances complexion
- Boost your immune system

Myrrh Oil:

Myrrh essential oil is valued since centuries for its versatility and effectiveness. It has been used from medicinal to religious purposes. Myrrh is a reddish-brown dried sap from a thorny tree — Commiphora myrrha. It is a great option of wellness and aids in the following:
Cleansing of the mouth and throat
- Promotes a youthful-looking complexion
- Improves the health of your nails
- Promotes emotional balance
- Eases coughs and colds
- Soothes digestive discomfort
- Boosts immunity.

Neem Oil

Neem, also known as Azadirachta Indica or Margosa tree is an evergreen tree that is found chiefly in the Indian subcontinent. It has been one of the main ingredients of the Ayurveda medicines in India.

Its contribution to beauty care and skin medicines is unmatchable. The skin benefits from it in the following ways:

- Treats dry skin and wrinkles
- Stimulates collagen production
- Reduces scars
- Heals wounds
- Treats acne
- Minimize warts and moles
- treats acne
- Heals psoriasis
- Treats nail fungus
- Acts as an insect repellent

Neroli Oil

It is obtained from the flowers of bitter orange trees. It is also known as orange blossom oil. Along with its use in medicines, it is actively made a part of perfumes cream, lotion, massage oil, and candles. In aromatherapy, it soothes the person and relives him/her from stress. Neroli oil has antimicrobial, antifungal, and antioxidant properties. Seizures, depression, high blood pressure, menopausal symptoms all can be calmed with this oil. For the skin it serves the following purpose:

- Reduces acne and breakouts.
- Soothes irritation
- Accelerates the process of regeneration
- Improves sleep.
- Target acute inflammation
- Reduces sensitivity to pain.

Orange Oil

Orange essential oil is extracted from the rind of the sweet orange, Citrus sinensis, Often the leaves and flowers are also used to obtain orange oil. It is used for a variety of purposes some of them are:

- Boosts mood
- Reduces stress
- Treats acne
- Relieves stomach upset
- Fights Antimicrobial activity.
- Enhances skin complexion
- Improves the texture of the skin
- Gives radiance and smoothens the skin.

Patchouli Oil

Patchouli Oil has its origin lying in an aromatic herb. The leaves and stem of this plant are left to dry out and then the oil is extracted from it. It often plays a role as an additive in products like perfumes, cosmetics, and incense. Some of its uses worth mentioning are:
- Treats skin conditions such as dermatitis, acne, or dry, cracked skin.
- Relieves depression
- Eases symptoms of cold and headache
- Soothes headache
- Treats oily hair and dandruff

Peppermint Oil

Peppermint is usually found in North America and Europe. Its leaves contain the essence from which is extracted this useful oil. Peppermint essential oil is being used in aromatherapy since eras. Its soothing effect relaxes your mind and body. Its potential health benefits are:
- Treats various digestive issues
- Reduces the feeling of nausea
- Gives Relief from itching
- Treats headache
- Soothes muscle pain
- Used in mouthwash
- It is anti-inflammatory
- It is anti-bacterial
- Reduces acne
- Heals sunburn
- Stimulates hair growth

Rosemary Oil

Rosemary Essential Oil has myriad benefits for your skin. It is being used in folk medicine since centuries, and it is widely used to date in cosmetic products. To have this oil as a skincare product can do wonders for the health of your skin. The following are the few benefits:
- Increases circulation and blood flow, which results in healthy skin and glowing skin.
- Reduces hyperpigmentation.
- Anti-bacterial properties stimulate healing.
- Balances natural oils of the skin.
- Control wrinkles and aging.
- Reduce the appearance of under-eye circles and puffiness.
- Subside acne and breakouts.
- Induces hair growth.

CARRIER OILS & WHY ARE THEY NEEDED?

Carrier oils, as the name suggests, is a base oil which dilutes Essential oils and "carry" it to your skin. Essential oils are potent and strong in nature. Oils can only be diluted in oil therefore; carrier oil is a fine choice for this purpose. Their direct application on skin can cause irritation, unwanted reactions, and redness on your skin. Therefore, Essential oils needs to be diluted in carrier oils to reduce their concentration and can be applied on skin without causing any irritation or uneasiness. Carrier oils can directly be used on your skin. Other than being called vegetable oils, in natural skincare, these are also called fixed oils, base oils. Carrier oils are vegetable oils which are extracted from the fatty portion of a plant. The seeds, kernels, and nuts are the common source of extraction. Carrier oils are not volatile like Essential oils and do not tend to evaporate. They carry a faint scent which is usually nutty and sweet while, some are odorless.

I was certainly impressed when I read about the importance of carrier oils. I was familiar with their benefits but I wasn't aware that their weightage in aromatherapy and skincare is greater than that I had in my mind. I would recommend every reader to include the following carrier oils in their skincare regimes. These will give nourishment, radiance, glow, and flawlessness that we all desire. It gives your skin the missing health and lost elasticity. Some of these Carrier oils that are a must-have are:

TOP 5 PICKS FOR CARRIER OILS TO HAVE AT HOME

Jojoba Oil

Jojoba (pronounced as ho-h—ba) is listed under oil is actually a liquid wax. It is a golden yellow-colored oil-like wax that resembles our body's natural oil therefore, is absorbed well into our skin. It grows in the desert regions of Arizona, southern California, and Mexico. Jojoba is rich in eicosenoic acid, omega-9 fatty acid, vitamin C, vitamins B, vitamin E, copper, and zinc. Its oily composition makes it suitable to be used in conditioners and as a moisturizer. It has a long shelf-life. Jojoba oil is a little on the expensive side in terms of its price however, its benefits take over its price. The benefits are:

- Strengthens hair.
- Moisturizes hair follicles.
- Eliminates dryness.
- Treats dandruff.
- Hydrates skin.
- Turns skin shiny.

Coconut Oil:

Coconut oil is known as superfood. It is not only famous in the domain of natural skincare but in general, it is celebrated for its numerous and versatile health benefits. The unique combination of fatty acids has positive effects on your skin, hair, and health. While kept on room temperature its form remains solid and later wen warmed turns liquid. Coconut oil is free from the traces of no cholesterol and no fiber. It is rich in Vitamin E. Its properties are an antioxidant, antifungal, anti-inflammatory, and antibacterial agents.

Generations have benefitted from this fruit's properties as they are absorbed into the skin and improves its health. In olden days it was used for various purposes:

- A Medicine for Eczema.
- Protects your skin from UV rays, hydrates, and restores.
- Reduces inflammation.
- Helps in healing wounds.
- Protects the skin from harmful bacteria.
- Smoothens the skin.
- Prevents acne.
- Nourishes, repairs, strengthens, and protects hair.

Olive Oil

It is commonly found in households and used in kitchens. On tropical use it is thicker and oilier in nature. It is rich in antioxidants and phenol, effective in soothing the skin. Oleic acid, one of its main components, plays a role in improving heart and cardiovascular system. Homer referred to it as 'liquid gold.' It's being used to date and will be used for the longest time. It is rich in Vitamin E, A, D, and K, Omega-3 and Omega-6. Olive oil is being used worldwide to ensure the health of your skin, nails, and hair. Some of the health benefits are:

- It improves complexion.
- It gives elasticity to your skin.
- It moisturizes skin and scalp.
- It is anti-aging.
- It is an antioxidant.
- It is used in treating Eczema and psoriasis.
- It improves healing.
- It exfoliates the skin.
- It reduces dandruff.
- It subsides scalp irritation.
- It leaves your hair smooth and soft.

Sweet Almond Oil

Sweet almond oil effectively moisturizes skin and nourishes it with its high level of Vitamin A. It also has vitamin D and E in abundance which leaves dry skin soft and conditioned. It also holds in itself Omega-3 Fatty acids and zinc. As compared to Olive Oil, this oil is more scentless, and will not interfere with the aroma of the essential oil. However, it needs to be stored in the refrigerator, while the other oils can be stored under room temperature. Its benefits are:

- Reduces under eye circles.
- Improves skin complexion.
- Treats dry skin.
- Improves acne.
- Reverses sun damage.
- Reduces scars.
- Reduces stretch marks.

Avocado Oil

Avocado oil is a think-green colored heavy edible oil. It has a sufficient amount of oleic acid, a mono-saturated fatty acid that helps treating dry and damaged skin. It is also considered as an excellent source of antioxidants, essential fatty acids, minerals, and vitamins. It smoothly absorbs in your skin. Following are the ways in which it can treat the skin:

- Soothes itchy and irritating skin
- Heals chapped skin
- Hydrates skin
- Rejuvenates dry skin
- Protects skin from ultra-violet rays.

WARNING: Mineral Oils Are NOT Carrier Oils

Nowadays, many companies are using mineral oils as a substitute for carrier oils since it's significantly cheaper, and they're mostly used in baby oils and commercially available moisturizers. However, these petroleum byproducts will clog skin pores and prevent your skin from absorbing essential oil. Therefore, choose and research before buying these oils. Buy from an authentic source or shop.

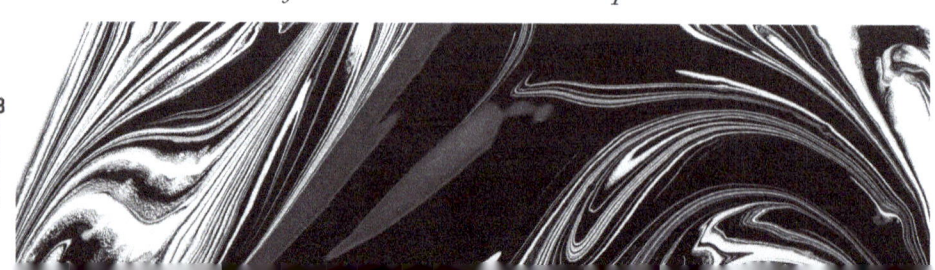

THE CONCEPT OF SYNERGY BLENDS

After excessive result I found another interesting dimension that essential oils carry. I was intrigued to come across the process of synergy where multiple components of a system come together to produce an overarching effect that cannot be reduced to the simple adding up of each individual effect. Synergy means to create something that is greater as a whole than the sum of its parts.

In aromatherapy, to give people an experience worth remembering synergy blends are created by blending different essential oils in correct ratios. These oils together work better in creating an intensified effect that could not have been achieved with the use of oils individually. They are normally crafted by aromatherapists, chemists, lab technicians, and other R&D professionals as both expertise and creativity is required for a synergy blend to be both effective and pleasing to the senses.

When different essential oils are blended or mixed, the interaction between its various constituents can also give rise to these incredible synergistic effects. For example, it has been shown that the antifungal properties of Tea Tree oil (Melaleuca alternifolia) and Lavender oil (Lavandula angustifolia) are potentiated when mixed together.

You must be wondering what makes Synergy Blends special. Well. There are two aspects in which we can understand the valuable effects which synergy blends give. One is the interaction between the various essential oil constituents. Different essential oils with their different properties come together and complement each other's effects and creating a powerful impact when used.

As a result, the benefits of using a synergy blend exceed the benefits of using the individual oils by themselves.

CHEMICAL FAMILY	EXAMPLE CONSTITUENTS	REPUTED EFFECT(S)	FOUND IN
Monoterpenes	• Limonene • Pinene • Myrcene • Camphene • Ocimene	• Antifungal • Antibacterial • Antispasmodic • Expectorant • Anti-inflammatory • Antinociceptive	• Grapefruit • Orange • Neroli • Eucalyptus • Pine
Sesquiterpenes	• Chamazulene • Caryophyllene • Farnesene • Bisabolene • Humulene	• Anti-inflammatory • Antibacterial • Antifungal • Anxiolytic • Antispasmodic • Antioxidant	• German Chamomile • Myrrh • Patchouli • Cedarwood • Ginger
Alcohols	• Nerol • Geraniol • Citronellol • Menthol • Santalol	• Antibacterial • Antifungal • Stimulating • Anti-inflammatory	• Geranium • Rosewood • Vetiver • Patchouli

CHEMICAL FAMILY	EXAMPLE CONSTITUENTS	REPUTED EFFECT(S)	FOUND IN
Esters	• Geranyl acetate • Bornyl acetate • Linalyl acetate • Eugenyl acetate	• Calming • Sedative • Antifungal • Antispasmodic • Anti-inflammatory	• Roman Chamomile • Jasmine • Geranium • Ylang Ylang
Aldehydes	• Neral • Citral • Citronellal • Cinnamaldehyde	• Calming • Sedative • Antiseptic • Relaxes muscles • Anti-inflammatory	• Melissa • Cinnamon • May Chang • Lemongrass
Ketones	• Camphor • Thujone • Carvone • Fenchone • Piperitone	• Sedative • Relieves pain • Relaxes muscles • Thins mucus • Can be neurotoxic	• Sage • Wormwood • Rosemary • Fennel • Spearmint
Phenols	• Carvacrol • Eugenol • Safrole	• Antibacterial • Antifungal • Relieves pain • Relaxes muscles • Can irritate skin / respiratory linings	• Thyme • Clove • Cinnamon • Oregano
Oxides	• Cineol • Bisabolol oxide A • Bisabolol oxide B	• Antibacterial • Antiviral • Expectorant • Thins mucus • Stimulating	• Eucalyptus • German Chamomile • Rosemary • Tea Tree

Essential Oil Constituents and Their Reputed Effects

It is important to note that the mapping between specific constituents and their effects is not always one-to-one; not all constituents will display the reputed effects for each of the chemical families listed above. Instead, these are overarching, generalized effects that tend to be observed in certain groups of constituents. In a synergy, it is believed that some of these effects 'come together' to enhance one another.

Fragrance matters to all of our senses. It is one of the please qualities that allure us towards anything that has an appealing scent. While we blend different essential oils that complement each other to give the best results for our mind and body we cannot forget to balance their fragrance. Blending can sometimes allow the scent to overpower others resulting in repelling the user from making it a part of his practice. The fragrances of all the individual oil should be balanced and in harmony with each other. This is where fragrance notes are taken into consideration.

A Frenchman called Piesse classified the odors of essential oils in the 19th century according to musical scales, and this is where the top, middle, and base notes originated. As a rule of thumb, the combination between top, middle, and base notes should be in harmony and the following formula is normally used. Select oils from all three categories but use less of the top and middle notes than that of the base note.

There are some "rules" that people like to mention, and these will be the guiding source that will help in producing a standard well-rounded fragrance: Top notes 15 - 25% of the blend. Middle notes 30 - 40% of the blend. Base notes 45 - 55% of the blend example - you would use 4 drops of Geranium (middle note) with 3 drops of Eucalyptus (top note) and 5 drops of Ylang Ylang (base note).

Essential Oil Blending Chart Example

BASE	Agarwood, Angelica, Cedar-wood, Vetiver, Sandalwood, patchouli, Frankincense, Myrrh
MIDDLE	camomile, cinnamon Clove, Clary Sage, Canola, Jasmin, Rosemary, Rosewood, Tea tree, Germanium
TOP	Citronella, Cassia, Bergamot, Basil, Grapefruit, Lemon, Lemongrass, Spearmint, Orange, pepermint, Eucalyptus

The perfect blend and mixture of oils will give you the required nutrients and properties which are beneficial for your health and serves the purpose effectively.

Queens' Secrets' Synergy Essential Oil Blends

Synergy Essential Oil	Key Ingredients
Tranquilize	A mix of lavender, petitgrain, grapefruit and ylang ylang
Pain Relief	A mix of pine, eucalyptus, peppermint, rosemary.
Brilliance	A mix of rosewood, bergamot, lemon, orange, tangerine, palmarosa and vetiver
Relaxation	A mix of ylang ylang, lavender, myrrh, rosewood, tangerine, and bergamot
Sensuality	A mix of ylang ylang, bergamot, myrrh, rosewood, rose geranium, and patchouli
Serenity	A mix of lavender, orange, tangerine, rosewood, rose geranium, and chamomile
Vitality	A mix of frankincense, palmarosa, lavender, bergamot, cypress, geranium, and sage

CHAPTER 03
NUMINOUS CHINA

Goodbye Blackheads & Open Pores Mask/ 37
Ginger Honey Mask/ 37
Ginseng & Green Tea Mask/ 38
Chinese Empress Pearl Mask/ 39
Chinese Green Papaya Mask/ 40
Mung Bean Face Mask for Acne/ 41
Anti-Ageing Mung bean Face Mask/ 42
Glowing Skin with Almond/ 42
Ancient Chinese Empress Herbal Bath/ 43

CHAPTER 03
NUMINOUS CHINA

My trip to China fascinated and brought me closer to their unique ancient homecare skin rituals, which they celebrate to date. Chinese medicine is primarily influenced by herbs and roots that are rich in minerals, vitamins, and other natural qualities, which results in radiant and glowing skin.

China's Empresses commissioned the best doctors to treat skin problems from burn spots to wrinkles. Empress Wu (625-705) was the famous Empress in Chinese history whose youthful skin was talked about even at the age of 80. Her flawless skin's beauty's secret lied in her famous recipe called "fairy powder". The "Fairy powder" was a combination of green tea extract, mung beans, and Chinese Motherwort (picked on the 5th day of the fifth lunar month). The religious application of the powder every morning and evening gave her the skin that made its place in history.

Another Empress named Empress Dowager Cixi is famous for her beauty throughout the world. She had also set up an imperial medical department to research skincare remedies which give us an insight into her interest in this domain. Personally, she used a powder made of pearls which are rich in calcium and gives an even skin tone. Moreover, her skin cream made of flower distillate was to maintain her beauty and glow. Along with this her beauty care routine included the use of Egg white, jade roller, and flower extracts. These are all health-enhancing products which she carried out to keep her beauty intact.

There was another lady whose skincare routine impressed me and is worth mentioning is the famous Chinese Mistress called Yang Yuhuan. She is not only known for her beauty but also managed to be the favourite wife of the Emperor (Xuanzong) in the Tang dynasty. She is known to be among the "Four great beauties" of China. Her luminous skin was a result of skincare which was made by combining goji berries, almond oil, and honey. In Chinese medicine Gogi berries (called Wolfberries by the Chinese) were used to treat skin problems that were linked to abnormalities in the liver and blood. These contain vitamin C and beta carotene to heal and nourish the liver and blood. Her regime also included the use of litchi, rich in protein, vitamin B and C, phosphorus, and iron, in which she submerged her body in a regular hot spring bath. She enhanced her beauty with this regime and her skin remained softened, smooth, glowing, and young.

Bei Qi, Huang Qi, and Goji are three herbs that are explicitly used in Chinese beauty care. Bei Qi is known for improving skin clarity; Huang Qi is excellent for revitalizing tired, aging skin; and Goji is known to defend skin against aging. Furthermore, another way the women from Chinese origin hydrated and provided nutrients to their skin is by steeping herbs in hot water and keep a regular intake of herbal tea. These detox your body and resultantly amplifying skin's health, complexion, and glow.

The Jade Roller is an ancient roller or stone that is used regularly by Chinese women. It is believed to have the same effect as that of dry brushing your body. This natural stone regulates the blood circulation and opens up meridian blockage allowing your Qi [Chi] and blood circulation to flow well. Jade is known for soothing, de-puffing, and decreasing wrinkles leaving you with youthful skin. The Chinese women's skin experiences the following:

- Protects your skin from UV rays, hydrates, and restores.
- Reduces inflammation.
- Helps in healing wounds.
- Protects the skin from harmful bacteria.
- Smoothens the skin.
- Prevents acne.

One of the main ingredients used in Chinese skincare and beauty regime is Mung Beans, also known as Green Gram. These are pulses widely used in the continent of Asia. Mung beans are rich in antioxidants such as flavonoids, phenolic acids, cinnamic acid, and caffeic acid. These prevent radical damage, chronic inflammation, cardiac arrest, and cancer. Natural ingredients and properties have the ability to fight the foreign entities in the body and boost your immune system. Mung beans are known to have anti-inflammatory properties which reduce high blood pressure and thirst. The said reductions prevent the body from being hit or affected by heatstroke. Antioxidants ease and lower the heat stress in the body. It further reduces the level of bad cholesterol and resultantly risk of heart disease as well. Similarly, these assist in regular bowel movements and the maintenance of digestive health.

Whereas skin is concerned Mung beans with their magic, have been enhancing the beauty, health, and texture of the skin. The abrasive texture of it helps in exfoliation of the skin. Dead cells, dust, dirt particles can be removed through exfoliation with mung beans. Mung beans help in unveiling the freshness lying hidden underneath the skin. Moreover, its properties treat acne, removes suntan, and rejuvenates the skin. Skin damaged from the UV rays and pollution can be made better with the consistent use of Mung beans can recover your original skin health and complexion. The process of slowing down of premature ageing by increasing the production of elastin and collagen in your body to keep your skin young with the use of these pulses. Mung beans have been doing wonders for skin since ages, and they continue to spread their magic till today.

Another major ingredient widely used in Chinese beauty regime is ginger. It is considered to be a superfood catering to various health issues. More than 40 anti-oxidants are present in it which fights the prominent and recurring signs of ageing. The intake of ginger in any form flushes out toxins from the body and improves blood circulation. Both of the said activities help your skin to heal and glow from within. Free radicals causing other skin issues can be curbed with the use of ginger. The antiseptic properties make it a natural product to fight bacteria. It treats recurring breakouts and stubborn acne.

Have you been worried about the scars left due to pigmentation? Your skin looks patchy and dull. In such times, treat your skin with ginger. The antioxidant properties soften the skin and reduce the marks leaving your skin even-toned and revitalized. Ginger is one of the most appreciated natural products in the world of beauty and skincare. Making it a part of your routine can do wonders for your skin and hair.

GOODBYE BLACKHEADS & OPEN PORES MASK

INGREDIENTS	
Mung Beans Powder	2 ts
Oatmeal Powder	4 ts
Green Tea Power	2 ts
Myrrh Essential	8 drop
Distilled Water	

DIRECTION

1. Mix all dry ingredients with distilled water in either one-one or half ratio till you get a soft and watery paste. Then you can add myrrh oil.
2. You may directly apply it on your face or use a face mask sheet on your skin and apply the mask over the mask sheet.
3. Rinse well with warm water after 15 minutes.

I recommend applying the products that contain propolis to boost anti-inflammation and skin immunity.

 MIX  APPLY TO FACE  RINSE AFTER 15 MIN

GINGER HONEY MASK

This ginger honey face mask recipe will make your skin look radiant! It will help tighten and tone, as well as aid in reducing pore size, discoloration, inflammation, and the bacteria that cause blemishes.

INGREDIENTS	
fresh squeezed Lemon Juice	3 ts
Raw Honey	4 ts
Ginger Powder	3 ts
Cinnamon essential oil	8 drop

DIRECTION

1. Combine all ingredients in a medium-sized bowl to form a thick paste.
2. The paste should have a consistency that sticks to your skin. Add lemon juice or other ingredients as necessary to reach your desired thickness.
3. Apply the paste to your entire face and neck areas.
4. After 20 minutes, rinse off the mask and pat dry.
5. You may use any skin tuner that you normally use after the rinse.

 MIX  APPLY TO FACE  RINSE AFTER 15 MIN

---———————————— *About raw honey* ————————————

Raw honey helps balance the bacteria on your skin, which makes it a great product to use for acne. It has been studied as an anti-acne product and found to be significantly more effective than other popular products. Honey speeds up your skin cells' healing processes.

Used cosmetically or topically in general, Cinnamon Essential Oil is reputed to calm dry skin, effectively alleviate aches, pains, and stiffness in the muscles and joints, address acne, rashes, and infections, enhance circulation, nourish the skin, slow the look of aging, and revive the skin tone.

Lemons are rich in vitamin C and citric acid, so they can help brighten and lighten your skin when used over time. Vitamin C is a great antioxidant for neutralizing free radicals and boosting collagen production.

GINSENG & GREEN TEA MASK

This easy to made recipe relies on the nutrients of ginseng which heal and nourish the skin by stimulating cell growth and extending cellular life span.

Avocado is added for its nourishing and skin softening qualities. This recipe is best for normal to dry and mature skins, and is easy to prepare.

INGREDIENTS

Mashed Avocado	1/2 or 90gr
Chinese or Korean ginseng root liquid or ginseng powder dissolved in hot water	1/4 tsp
Wheat Germ Oil	1/4 tsp
Green Tea Powder	1/2 tsp
Pure Tea Tree or Vetiver Essential oil	3 drops

DIRECTION

1. Blend all ingredients together using a pestle and mortar or put in the blender until you have a creamy paste.
2. Spread over face, neck, and décolletage twice a week in the evening, ideally whilst in the bath when the skin is pre-warmed. Leave on for 10-15 minutes, then wash off and moisturize.

You may apply it to the backs of your hands as a wonderful hand treatment. It leaves the hands super soft and refined with young-looking.

MIX

APPLY TO FACE

APPLY TO HAND

RINSE AFTER 10-15 MIN

In Traditional Chinese medicine (TCM,) ginseng is known as an energy tonic which replaces lost ch'i to the meridians and organs. Native to China, Japan and Korea, ginseng is believed to help alleviate stress-related conditions, combat fatigue and introduce vital energy or ch'l into the body. In this recipe ginseng combined with green tea, it works to detoxify and restore health and radiance to the skin, as well as reduce skin's redness.

Wheat germ oil is extracted from the germ of the wheat kernel, when applied to the skin, delivers a healthy infusion of vitamin A, vitamin D, B vitamins, antioxidants, and fatty acids. In particular, wheat germ oil is a rich source of vitamin E, which helps reduce skin damage, fight free radicals, support healthy collagen formation and maintain even skin tone.

CHINESE EMPRESS PEARL MASK

The very fine and gentle paste-like mix of this recipe, that have been reported to be used by Ching Dynasty Empress Dowager almost 2000 year ago, has a fabulous result. The ancient combination used human milk which was easily available in the Chinese palace from nursing nannies. This mask recipe has been created With more modern interactions.

INGREDIENTS		DIRECTION
pearl powder or eggshell powder from one egg	1 tsp	1. Mix all ingredients together into a paste.
2. Dab and massage the mask gently into the skin after cleansing process.
3. Leave for at least 15 minutes and allow to dry to tighten and firm the skin. Wash off with cool water.

Tone the skin with rosewater and apply moisturizer. For maximum benefits, this mask should be used at least twice a week before bedtime. |
fresh cow's milk or soy milk	1/2 tsp	
fresh lemon juice	1/2 ts	
rice bran powder	1/2 tsp	
Geranium essential oil (optional)	5 drops	

MIX

APPLY TO SKIN

WASH AFTER 15 MIN

Fresh pearls when gathered, crushed and applied to the skin to clarify texture and reduce aging spots. Enriched in proteins, essential amino acids and calcium, pearls were also taken internally to detoxify and regulate the body system.

Eggshell membranes contain healing nutrients like hyaluronan, so your rough, peeling cuticles will be healthy and soft by the next day. Freshen up your skin with this inexpensive mask: Finely crush one or two eggshells, whisk together with one egg white, and apply all over your face.

Milk also contains retinol, a known anti-aging and skin-restoring antioxidant. Plus, milk's vitamin D is also an anti-aging vitamin thanks to its anti-inflammatory effects and protection from UV rays.

CHINESE GREEN PAPAYA MASK

This is a quite active mask, so I will not recommend it for a sensitive skin, but it has an amazing anti-aging and softening effects on dry to normal skin type.

INGREDIENTS		DIRECTION

mashed green papaya pulp (You may use ripe papaya if you can't find the green one)	1/4 cup	1. Blend all the ingredients together to the paste.
white clay powder	2 tbsp	2. Apply it on your face and neck.
honey	1/2 tbsp	3. Allow the ingredients to their magic job on your skin for 15 minutes. Rinse with warm water and apply your regular moisturiser.
pure rose hip essential oil (optional)	5 drops	The ideal usage of this mask is once a week.
almond oil	1 tsp	

MIX

APPLY TO FACE

RINSE AFTER 15 MIN

Papaya will help to dissolve and removed damaged and dead skin from the face because of its papain enzyme along with the alpha-hydroxy acids which acts as a powerful exfoliator. Papaya has also the skin lightening properties that help clear blemishes and pigmentation. Almond oil has been used for centuries to treat dry skin conditions, including eczema and psoriasis. Improves acne. The oil's fatty acid content may help dissolve excess oil on the skin, while the retinoid in the oil may reduce the appearance of acne and improve cell turnover. Helps reverse sun damage.

MUNG BEAN FACE MASK FOR ACNE

The deep cleansing and exfoliating properties of mung bean powder will help get rid of and prevent further acne.

INGREDIENTS	
mung bean powder	1 tsp
turmeric	1/3 tsp
yogurt	1,1/2 ts

DIRECTION

1. In a bowl, mix all the ingredients until you get a soft and creamy paste.
2. Using clean fingers, gently slather this face mask mixture, avoiding the areas around the eyes and mouth.
3. Leave the mask on for about 3 to 5 minutes or until it dries up completely.
4. Use warm/tepid water to rinse off the mask completely.

MIX

APPLY TO SKIN

WASH AFTER 3-5 MIN

In Chinese Medicine, Mung beans are described as nutritious food and medicine for the body. It is also a great detox food that helps clear heat and toxins from the body, thereby helping treat acne and promote clear skin from within.

Yogurt is anti-inflammatory properties which will soothe acne inflammation and redness. Its skin lightening properties will fade away acne scars and blemishes. Yogurt also has antibacterial properties which will fight off acne causing germs.

Turmeric acts as an antibacterial and anti-inflammatory agent when applied topically to skin. It will reduce acne redness and inflammation on the skin as well as prevent more acne.

ANTI-AGEING MUNG BEAN FACE MASK

This mung bean face mask contains green tea which makes it an excellent anti-aging face mask. Applying green tea topically helps tighten, firm and lift skin. Green tea will also water and plump up dry skin, thereby making skin smooth, soft and youthful.

INGREDIENTS

mung bean powder	1 tsp
green tea	1,1/2 tsp

DIRECTION

1. Brew Green Tea and let it cool down
2. Add mung bean powder in a small bowl and mix it with green tea to form a paste.
3. Gently apply this paste onto your face using clean fingers.
4. Wait for the face mask to dry up.
5. When it dries up completely, rinse off with tepid water and pat dry.

BREW TEA

MIX

APPLY TO FACE

RINSE AFTER IT DRIES

GLOWING SKIN WITH ALMOND

This face mask will help to remove the dull colour, brown spots, acne and fine wrinkle from the skin.

INGREDIENTS

Almond	100 gr
Egg White	1
Rosehip essential oil	3 drops

DIRECTION

1. Soak almond in warm water, remove the brown coat and ground it into a cream.
2. Whisk the egg.
3. Mix the egg white and almond cream with Rosehip essential oil
4. Apply the paste on your face and decollate for 30 minutes and rinse off with cold water

MIX

APPLY TO SKIN & DECOLLATE

WASH AFTER 30 MIN

ANCIENT CHINESE EMPRESS HERBAL BATH

The deep cleansing and exfoliating properties of mung bean powder will help get rid of and prevent further acne.

INGREDIENTS

Mung Beans	10 gr
Lilly Buds	10 gr
Borneol	10 gr
Talk	30 gr
Monkshood	30 gr
Dahurian Angelica Root	30 gr
Sandalwood	30 gr
Resin	30 gr

DIRECTION

Grind all ingredients and pour directly into your hot bathtub. Soak for 30 minutes

SOAK IN TUB

SOAK FOR 30 MIN

CHAPTER 04
REGAL INDIA

Sacred Neem in Indian Beauty Routine/ 47
Neem Hair Mask/ 48
Indian Whitening Exfoliation Mask/ 48
Mango Mousse Cream/ 49
Acne Scars Treatment/ 50
Multani Mitti in Indian Beauty Care/ 51
AMLA, Perfect Hair's Secret/ 53

After China, my interest in natural skincare and spa ownership urged me to get familiarity with the Indian skincare. India is rich in natural ingredients that are essential for improving skin life and quality. The bridal and wedding culture of India caught my attention to the extent that I attended a few weddings to comprehend the bridal beauty care rituals. The grand celebrations, colors, and affection towards the bride during weddings is unparalleled. The brides are treated like goddesses. The grandeur of their dresses and jewelry speaks for their involvement and scale of the celebration of a wedding. Women are bathed in pure milk, and Ubtan is applied to enrich their complexion and radiance. Ubtan is a traditional paste that consists of rosewater, turmeric, milk, milk cream, lemon juice, gram flour, and almond powder. This is applied for days before the marriage to give a luminous and brilliant skin texture. In India, turmeric is one of the basic elements of natural skincare products. Ladies rely on its healing properties to prevent their skin from aging and dullness. It further benefits the skin with the following

- Exfoliates the skin.
- Remove dead skin cell
- Nourish your skin
- Reduces hyperpigmentation
- Replenishes your skin
- Exterminates acne

SACRED NEEM IN INDIAN BEAUTY ROUTINE

Neem is probably the king of all other beauty ingredients Indians have out there. Each and every part of this magical plant is beneficial in some way.

Take a few Neem leaves and boil them in the water. Let it cool down and then dip a cotton ball into it and evenly rub it all over your face. This is great to treat acne.

Mix 1 tablespoon of Neem Powder, One tablespoon of Yogurt and 2 tablespoon of cucumber juice (or one tablespoon of mashed cucumber). Apply this mask on you face and neck and rinse off after 20 minutes. This mask is perfect to reduce oiliness of your face.

Place a small amount of Neem oil on the tips of your fingers and gently massage into the scalp and hair roots. Work the oil into the ends if desired and leave on for at least 60 minutes. For added benefits, you may leave the oil in your hair overnight. Cover your hair and lay a towel over your pillow while you sleep, as the oil will stain.

Due to its antibacterial, antifungal and anti-inflammatory properties, neem is excellent to curb dandruff and treats hair loss. It helps the hair follicles to become stronger and also encourages hair growth.

Mix two teaspoon of neem powder with few drops of rose water to make a smooth paste. Apply it on your face and neck and post 15 minutes wash it off. Neem will clear out blemishes and marks on the skin and the rosewater will act as a natural toner to shrink the pores.

In order to cleanse skin of dirt, reduce breakouts and make your skin glow, mix equal amounts of papaya pulp made from a ripe papaya and neem powder. Apply the mask generously to your face and neck. After 30 minutes, rinse it off with cold water.

NEEM HAIR MASK

INGREDIENTS		DIRECTION
Fresh washed Neem Leaves	15-20	1. Add Neem leaves to a blender, add some water to it and blend until it forms a smooth paste.
or		
Neem powder	2 tbs	2. If you use neem powder, mix the powder with water and make a paste.
coconut oil	2 tbs	3. Place a bowl in casserole with some boiling water and transfer the neem paste to this bowl. (Do not place a paste in a casserole directly)
		4. Add the coconut oil to this paste and keep stirring continuously until the paste changes colour and becomes darker.
		5. Apply this mask all over hair and scalp and massage for a couple of minutes.
		6. Leave it on for about 30 to 40 minutes and wash off as usual.

MIX   APPLY TO HAIR   WASH AFTER 30-40 MIN

INDIAN WHITENING EXFOLIATION MASK

This mask is a great combination to boost skin's moisture. It Hydrate and brightens the skin. It increase elasticity and reduce fine lines and wrinkles. It can be applied on either face, under eyes or body. In case, you want to apply it on your body you may double or triple the amount of ingredients.

INGREDIENTS		DIRECTION
Gram Flour	3 tbs	1. Mix all the ingredients
Plain, Unflavoured Yogurt	3 tbs	2. Apply it on your face and neck for 15 minutes.
Turmeric Powder	2 ts	3. You may massage your face and neck with circular motion for 2 to 3 minutes
Sandalwood Powder	1 tbs	4. After 15 minutes rinse it with warm water.
Fresh Squeezed Lemon Juice	1 tbs	
Sandalwood Essential Oil	8 drops	
Whole Milk if your paste is too hard	2 tbs	

MIX   APPLY TO FACE & NECK AND MASSAGE FOR 3 MIN   WASH AFTER 15 MIN

About ingredients

Gram flour has certain properties that treat acne and has been used for this purpose in India for centuries. For one, the zinc in besan has been shown to fight the infections that cause your face to erupt with acne. Secondly, it also helps control excess sebum production and soothes inflamed skin

Sandalwood powder has long been used for skin problems and with good reason. Regular use of this powder can fight acne, exfoliate the skin, soothe sunburn, remove suntan, and reduce signs of aging like dry skin and wrinkles.

Yogurt, whether the Greek or regular kind, also contains lactic acid, an organic compound like zinc, calcium and B vitamins that aids in diminishing the appearance of wrinkles and fine lines by tightening, lightening and shrinking pores. Meanwhile, adding yogurt to your skin care regimen helps moisturize your skin and delay the signs of aging.

As an antiseptic and astringent, it also helps to clean the pores and reduce inflammation from mild skin irritations. What's more, studies have shown that sandalwood helps with skin conditions like acne, eczema, and psoriasis. In fact, many skincare products contain sandalwood oil as a key, age-fighting ingredient!

Turmeric contains antioxidants and anti-inflammatory components. These characteristics may provide glow and luster to the skin. Turmeric may also revive your skin by bringing out its natural glow You may want to try a turmeric face mask at home to see if the spice has any positive effects on your skin.

MANGO MOUSSE CREAM

This mask is a great combination to boost skin's moisture. It Hydrate and brightens the skin. It increase elasticity and reduce fine lines and wrinkles. It can be applied on either face, under eyes or body.In case, you want to apply it on your body you may double or triple the amount of ingredients.

INGREDIENTS		DIRECTION
Mango Butter	1 cup (cut-up)	1. Take a pot and fill it about 1/4 of the way with water. Set that pot on the stove to boil. Once the water begins to boil, take it off the heat and set aside.
Apricot Oil	1/2 cup	
Lavender Essential Oil	10 drops	2. Place your cut-up mango butter, apricot oil and essential oils in a glass container. Place your glass container into your pot of boiling water that you set aside in step one.
Geranium Essential Oil	5 drops	
Chamomile Essential Oil	5 drops	3. Using the back of a spoon or a fork, work your butter and oils into a paste.
Pink Mica (optional, add this at the very end)	1/4 ts	4. Fold in the pink mica powder and stir well to ensure the color is uniform.

5. To add volume and give it a fluffy consistency, whip the paste with an electric mixer on high for several minutes until it has increased in volume and is a bit stiff.
6. Scoop the Whipped Mango Mousse into your final containers and store in a cool place away from direct sun.

MIX

APPLY TO FACE & NECK AND MASSAGE FOR 3 MIN

WASH AFTER 15 MIN

---- *About ingredients* ----

Mango Butter is non-comedogenic. Mango Butter contains essential fatty acids and antioxidants that make it a wonderful choice for mature skin as well. The rich, nourishing nature of this butter can even help benefit those suffering from skin conditions such as eczema or psoriasis.

Apricot Kernel Oil makes a non-greasy, enriching emollient. It can be applied directly to the skin as a revitalizing salve that soothes and prevents acne, inflammation, and dryness. Used under the eyes, it is known to diminish the appearance of dark circles, fine lines, and puffiness.

Lavender oil is an essential oil derived from the lavender plant. It can be taken orally, applied to the skin, and breathed in through aromatherapy. Lavender oil can benefit the skin in numerous ways. It has the ability to lessen acne, help lighten skin, and reduce wrinkles.

Comprising powerful anti-inflammatory and calming properties, Chamomile Essential Oil is a wonder ingredient to help soothe your complexion. Whether it's rosacea, irritation, acne or any other skin concerns, Chamomile Oil is a great natural remedy to calm your skin

Used cosmetically or topically in general, Geranium Essential Oil is reputed to effectively eliminate dead cells, tighten the skin, promote the regeneration of new skin, and diminish signs of aging. Used medicinally, Geranium Essential Oil works as an anti-inflammatory and anti-septic agent.

ACNE SCARS TREATMENT

This face mask helps reduce acne and any resulting scars. The anti-inflammatory qualities can target your pores and calm the skin.

INGREDIENTS		DIRECTION
Organic Chickpea Flour or Basin	2 tbs	1. Apply a paste to your face and neck and leave it for 20 minutes to dry. Rinse it with cold water.
Organic Milk or Yogurt (or enough to make a paste)	4 ts	2. You may repeat the treatment twice a week.
Organic Turmeric Powder	1 ts	
Lemon	1/2 ts	
Myrrh Essential Oil	10 drops	

---- *About ingredients* ----

Turmeric is also known to reduce scarring. This combination of uses may help your face clear up from acne breakouts. Besan is really useful as a tan removal agent when applied to skin. The greek yogurt contains lactic acid which is a natural antibiotic. It exfoliates the skin, helps boost collagen and prevent wrinkles. And lemon -bleaching agent, lighten dark scars and fights acne. Myrrh prevents ageing signs, fights against acne, reduce the appearance of pores and helps heal acne scars.

MULTANI MITTI IN INDIAN BEAUTY CARE ACNE SCARS TREATMENT

Multani mitti or Fuller's Earth named after the city of Multan where a dollop of lime clay was extracted on 18th century, and the inhabitants were surprised by its amazing cleansing properties. Its popularity rose so high that hundreds of years later, multani mitti has become a part of every household for a number of purposes like cooling the skin, fighting pimples, sunburn, skin rashes and infections along with Facilitates blood circulation, leading to radiant, glowing skin. This traditional skincare ingredient is rich in minerals, such as aluminium silicate, that effectively absorb oil, dirt, sweat and impurities, leaving the skin clean, soft and radiant.

TREAT OILY SKIN WITH MULTANI MITTI

This face mask helps reduce acne and any resulting scars. The anti-inflammatory qualities can target your pores and calm the skin.

INGREDIENTS	
Multani Mitti	2 ts
Rose Water	2 ts
Orange Peel Powder	2 ts

DIRECTION

1. Mix all ingredients till they form a smooth paste.
2. Apply this pretty-smelling pack on your face evenly and leave it on for 20 minutes.
3. Wash it off after it completely dries. Your skin will become smooth and oil-free.
4. Repeat this process at least thrice a week for best results.

MIX

APPLY TO FACE

WASH AFTER 20 MIN

GET RID OF EYES DARK CIRCLE WITH MULTANI MITTI

INGREDIENTS	
Potato	1/2 small
Multani Mitti	1 tbs
Coconut Oil	1 ts
Fresh Lemon Juice	1 ts

DIRECTION

1. Simply take half a potato and grate it.
2. Mix it with lemon juice, one teaspoon coconut oil and multani mitti.
3. Use this paste on your eyes and leave for twenty minutes.
4. Wash off and see a remarkable difference in your dark circles.
5. You may use this paste twice a week.

MIX

APPLY TO HAIR

WASH AFTER 30-40 MIN

SCRUB AND EXFOLIATE WITH MULTANI MITTI

INGREDIENTS		DIRECTION
Orange Peel Powder	1 ts	1. If you want to exfoliate your skin, there's nothing better than teaming all the above mentioned ingredients to the paste and use it circularly on your skin for radiant and glowing skin.
Sandalwood Powder	1 ts	
Gram Flour	1 ts	
Yogurt	1 tbs	2. Try the regime once or twice every week for best results.
Multani Mitti		

MIX

APPLY TO FACE & NECK

MULTANI MITTI FOR SPOT FREE SKIN

INGREDIENTS		DIRECTION
Tomato Juice	2 tbs	1. Make a paste by mixing all the ingredients.
Multani Mitti	2 tbs	2. Apply it on your face for 15 minutes before rinsing it with warm water.
Sandalwood Powder	1 ts	**Caution**: Tomato juice doesn't suit everybody so do a patch test on the underside of your wrist before using it in the face pack.
Turmeric Powder	1 ts	

MIX

APPLY TO FACE

WASH AFTER 15 MIN

MULTANI MITTI FOR FAIRNESS AND RADIANCE

INGREDIENTS

Multani Mitti — 2 ts

Honey — 2 ts

Papaya Pulp — 2 ts

DIRECTION

1. Mix a tablespoon each of multani mitti, honey, and papaya fruit pulp to form a paste.
2. Apply it evenly to your freshly washed face and remove it after it dries off completely.
3. Repeat it twice or thrice every week to obtain flawless skin.

MIX — APPLY TO FACE — REMOVE AFTER DREID

AMLA, PERFECT HAIR'S SECRET

CURRY LEAVES AND AMLA FOR HAIR GROWTH

INGREDIENTS

Curry Leaves — 1/4 cup

Chopped Amla — 1/4 cup

Coconut Oil — 1 cup

DIRECTION

1. Place a casserole half filled with water and place an empty bowl in it.
2. Pour coconut oil in a bowl and add the chopped amla and curry leaves to it.
3. Heat the oil until it turns brown.
4. Turn off the heat and set the oil aside to cool.
5. Collect the oil in a jar and discard the amla and curry leaves.
6. While it is still slightly warm, apply it to your scalp and hair. Massage your scalp for about 15 minutes.
7. Once you are done massaging your scalp and your hair is fully covered in the oil, wait for an additional 60 minutes.
8. Wash the oil out with a mild sulfate-free shampoo and cool/lukewarm water.

FOLLOW DIRECTION — APPLY TO HAIR & MASSAGE 15 MIN — WASH AFTER 60 MIN

---------- *Benefit* ----------

These are the ways you can use amla to stimulate hair growth. However, you need to keep certain points in mind before you use amla.

Curry leaves are antimicrobial, anti-inflammatory, antibacterial, antifungal, and antioxidant. They can improve scalp health and reduce hair fall. Curry leaves, when used with coconut oil, can help stimulate hair growth.

AMLA, HENNA AND SHIKAKAI FOR HAIR GROWTH

INGREDIENTS		DIRECTION
Amla Powder	2 tbs	1. Mix all the powders with water to get a smooth, consistent paste.
Henna Powder	2 tbs	2. Apply this paste as a hair mask to your hair and scalp.
Shikakai Powder	2 bs	3. Once your scalp and hair are fully covered, leave the mask on for about 40 minutes.
Water	-	4. Wash your hair with cool water. If you have relatively clean hair, you can skip shampooing as shikakai has cleansing properties.
		5. You may use this recipe once a week.

MIX — APPLY TO HAIR & SCALP — WASH AFTER 40 MIN

---------- *Benefit* ----------

Henna helps prevent dandruff and premature graying of hair and reduces hair fall while Shikakai,

Like amla, can stimulate hair growth and thickness and also strengthened the hair at the roots and improved hair health.

AMLA WITH EGG AND LEMON JUICE

INGREDIENTS		DIRECTION
Eggs	2 whole	1. Whisk the eggs in a bowl until they start to fluff up.
Amla Powder	1/2 cup	2. Add the amla powder, Amla juice and lemon juice to the bowl and stir until you get a smooth, consistent paste.
Amla Juice	3 tbs	3. Apply this paste as a hair mask to your hair and scalp.
Fresh Lemon Juice	2 tbs	4. Leave the mask on for about one hour.
		5. Wash your hair with cool water. Do not use warm/hot water as it may end up "cooking" the egg in your hair.

FOLLOW DIRECTION — APPLY TO HAIR & SCALP — WASH AFTER 60 MIN

Benefit

Eggs are often used in hair packs since they are full of protein. Egg yolk was shown to induce hair growth in human dermal cells. Lemon juice acts as a scalp cleanser and helps reduce dandruff because of its antibacterial, antifungal, and antiviral properties

GOLDEN PASTES WITH MAGICAL TURMERIC TO REDUCE STRETCH MARKS

INGREDIENTS

Turmeric	1 ts
Besan Powder	1 ts
Yogurt	2 tbs
Bitter Almond Oil	2 tbs

DIRECTION

1. Mix all the ingredients and apply on your stretch marks. Rub gently in circular motions for about 15 minutes.
2. Rinse well with water and apply bitter almond oil on the area.

MIX

APPLY TO STRETCH MARKS ABOUT 15 MIN

RINSE

TO REDUCE WRINKLES

INGREDIENTS

Turmeric	1 ts
Rice Powder	1 ts
Tomato Juice	2 tbs
Honey	1 ts
Raw Milk	1 tbs

DIRECTION

1. Mix all the ingredients to get smooth paste, apply it on your face, and leave it undisturbed till it dries.
2. Rinse off and apply your daily cream. You may use this twice a week.

FOLLOW DIRECTION

APPLY TO FACE

WASH AFTER DRIED

TO TREAT CRACKED HEELS

INGREDIENTS

Coconut Oil or Castor oOil	
Turmeric	

DIRECTION

1. Mix coconut oil or castor oil with turmeric.
2. Before taking bath apply this mixture to the cracked heels and leave for 15 minutes.

CHAPTER 05
ALLURING KOREA

JUDO Cleansing and Whitening Scrub/ 60
Korean Brightening Face Mask/ 61
Prank up Acne Mask/ 62
Mermaid Face Mask/ 63
Korean Inspired Rice Cream/ 64
Myeonyak Facial Medicine/ 65

CHAPTER 05

ALLURING KOREA

ALLURING KOREA

My research and interest intrigued and excited me to understand the Korean skincare regimes opted by women since ancient times. The Korean beauty ideal of a bright and radiant complexion is not a modern one. Since the olden days, white color in Korea is a symbol of spiritual purity. Therefore, white skin indicates purity, beauty, and high status. My visit to Korea revealed that during the Joseon dynasty, Confucianism gave ample importance and influenced women's beauty routines. It tells us that regardless of the class difference, every Joseon woman had the same desire to look beautiful by achieving a porcelain-like complexion and sporting a big, full hairdo. Also, it was thought that a women's clean skin and smooth was not only an indication of beauty but her inner purity as well.

In the Jangseogak Archives there are about 950 historic documents and manuscripts from the royal court that provide a vivid insight into the life and culture within the royal court which inform us what kinds of beauty products Joseon women used. It is explained that hwangmil or honey was applied to give luster to face and that jinyu or sesame oil was used to add shine to hair. There is also a mention of buying soseong, which is a special brush used for cleaning combs, for the court.

Koreans made their own lotions, scrubs, oils, and creams. One of the main ingredients in their skincare is Ground mung beans, these were powdered and turned into soaps and lotions were produced from the juice of plants. Since ages, vitamin E is being used to nourish the skin and its application is applauded by everyone in each era. To provide vitamin E to their skin Korean women added Safflower oil in their routine to have healthy and radiant skin. Another distinctive practice that Koreans practiced was inking their eyebrows to emphasize and enhance them. A facial cleanser that was widely used in the times of the Joseon dynasty is Jodu, a powdered soap with whitening properties. Rice and wheat grains were also used as they were rich in vitamin B which helps in repairing and brightening of the skin. During the Koyo Dynasty, the gisaeng (female entertainers of the royal court) and court ladies inked and drew thin eyebrows with powdered their faces generously. Rice water and mugwort facials are also prominent in Korean skincare. This practice not only aided women in olden days but women are to date enjoying the benefits it gives to their skin. Following the Korean beauty care regime will leave your skin rich, plush, and healthy. Some of the benefits all the above gave to their skin are:

- Skin tightening.
- Shrinks open pores.
- Anti-aging.
- Treats eczema and psoriasis.
- Heals the skin
- Exfoliates the skin

JUDO CLEANSING AND WHITENING SCRUB

The first step to achieving a beautiful porcelain-like complexion is to wash face clean. Jodu was the most common facial cleanser among Korean Royal ladies. This powdered soap would scrub off dead skin cells and reveal soft skin when rubbed onto wet face, and that it even has an excellent whitening effect.

INGREDIENTS

Mung Bean Powder	1 ts
Soybean Powder	1 ts
Adzuki beans (Red beans)	1 ts
Lavender or Geranium Essential Oil (optional)	5 drops

DIRECTION

1. Mix all the powder and add essential oil.
2. You may keep this powder in a container and keep it in your vanity cabinet.
3. Take a small amount of this powder and mix it with few drops of water and scrub circularly on your wet skin.
4. You might repeat it three times a week.

MIX

SCRAB ON WET SKIN

--- *Benefit* ---

Mung bean powder is a great cosmetic ingredient for clear skin, for it is described to be effective in preserving vitality and curing skin eruption, according to Donguibogam, a medical encyclopedia compiled during the Joseon period.

Adding Essential oil transform your unpleasant fishy smell powder into a pleasantly perfumed soap, which once upon a time was a luxury gift item for women in the court.

Although not every woman was fortunate enough to use expensive jodu, according to "Takjijeongrye" (a book of rules concerning the government's spending) and "Gyuhapchongseo" (encyclopedia of women's life) in the collection of the Jangseogak Archives at the Academy of Korean Studies, ordinary women, outside the royal court used to mix common cereal grains such as rice bran and wheat bran, which were wrapped in muslin or silk cloth, and rubbed onto the skin.

The milky-white water easily obtained from washing rice was also used in washing face.

KOREAN BRIGHTENING FACE MASK

This face mask is great to brighten your skin, fade pigmentation from your skin, and improve skin's texture and tone.

INGREDIENTS		DIRECTION
Mung Beans Powder	3 ts	1. Mix all dry ingredients with distilled water in either one to one or one to half ratio till you get a soft and gentle paste. Then you can add rose oil.
Rice Bran	2 ts	
Yulmu Powder	1 ts	2. You may directly apply it on your face or use a face mask sheet on your skin and apply the mask over the mask sheet.
Red Beans Power	1 ts	
Rose Oil	10 drops	3. Rinse well after 15 min and apply vitamin C serum to boost your skin's glow
Distilled Water		

MIX   APPLY TO FACE   RINSE AFTER 15 MIN

Benefit

The fine Yulmu seed powder offers gentle exfoliation that effectively removes dead skin cells that clog the pores. When lathered, the clay creates a dense and rich foam that contains papaya enzyme powder and kaolin clay and thoroughly cleanses makeup residue, impurities, and excess sebum inside the pores.

Mung bean not only are they a big part of the Chinese diet, but they've also been praised for helping to soothe acne and other skin ailments. This is achieved not by eating the legumes but by incorporating them into a face mask as they are rich in antioxidants and phytonutrients

Fine Grain Rice Bran Powder is gently exfoliating and is an old Japanese secret for smooth, soft skin. Rice Bran Powder is said to cleanse dirt and oil from pores, balance the natural oils while helping to moisturize the skin.

As a skincare ingredient red beans give the skin a shiny and radiant glow. They make the skin firm and silky, they're especially beneficial for oily skin. Of course, Japanese people don't just use the whole beans, they grind them into powder and mix with milk to wash their face or make them into face masks.

Rose Oil instead it has been proven as an excellent treatment for acne-prone skin due to its antiseptic and astringent properties. Its anti-inflammatory benefits will also help those that struggle with acne, inflammation, and/or skin redness.

PRANK UP ACNE MASK

INGREDIENTS		DIRECTION
Mung Bean Powder	3 ts	1. Mix all dry ingredients with distilled water in either one to one or one to one and a half ratio till you get a soft and gentle paste. Then you can add myrrh oil.
Oatmeal Powder	3 ts	
Kelp Powder	3 ts	2. You may directly apply it on your face or use a face mask sheet on your skin and apply the mask over the mask sheet.
Green Tea Power	2 ts	
Myrrh Essential Oil	10 drops	3. Rinse well with warm water after 15 minutes and apply your regular moisturising cream.
Distilled Water		

MIX

APPLY TO FACE

RINSE AFTER 15 MIN

―――― *Benefit* ――――

Kelps are large brown algae seaweeds that make up the order Laminariales. Sea Kelp Extract in skincare is perfect for anyone with dry and flaky patches of skin, due to its high iodine content. It is known to reduce the appearance of breakouts. Sea Kelp is also rich in antioxidants, which are known to help protect your skin against UVA rays, external aggressors, and daily pollution

Mung bean not only are they a big part of the Chinese diet, but they've also been praised for helping to soothe acne and other skin ailments. This is achieved not by eating the legumes but by incorporating them into a face mask as they are rich in antioxidants and phytonutrients

Oatmeal can soak up the excess oil on your skin and help treat acne. Its antioxidant and anti-inflammatory properties help to treat dry skin and remove dead skin cells. Oats also contain compounds called saponins, which are natural cleansers. They remove the dirt and oil that clog the pores and exfoliate the skin.

Green tea's anti-inflammatory properties can help reduce skin irritation, skin redness, and swelling. Applying green tea to your skin can soothe minor cuts and sunburn, too. Due to its anti-inflammatory properties, studies have also found topical green tea to be an effective remedy for many dermatological conditions.

Myrrh prevents aging signs, fights against acne, reduces the appearance of pores, and helps heal acne scars.

MERMAID FACE MASK

INGREDIENTS

Green Tea	3 tbs
Green tea leaves powder	1 tbs
Fresh squeezed lemon juice	1 ts
Bergamot Essential Oil	8 drops
Seaweed Strips (Sushi's main ingredient)	
Warm Water	

DIRECTION

1. Mix green tea and lemon juice and bergamot and add green tea leaves.
2. Soak your seaweed sheets in the above mixture for about 10-15 seconds until they are soft.
3. Place the sheets on your face and neck.
4. Leave it for 15 minutes and then remove the strips and wash your face with normal water.
5. This mask works amazing for oily and acne-prone skin types.

FOLLOW DIRECTION — APPLY TO FACE & NECK — WASH AFTER 15 MIN

Benefit

Green tea's anti-inflammatory properties can help reduce skin irritation, skin redness, and swelling. Applying green tea to the skin can soothe minor cuts and sunburn, too. Due to its anti-inflammatory properties, studies have also found topical green tea to be an effective remedy for many dermatological conditions.

The same mix of vitamins, minerals, fatty acids, and antioxidants that can benefit your body when you eat seaweed can also help your skin when you apply seaweed to it. The antioxidants in seaweed can help prevent free radical damage to the skin and protect against skin aging. In addition, seaweed can moisturize and calm the skin.

Lemons are rich in vitamin C and citric acid, so they can help brighten and lighten your skin when used over time. When it mix with green tea, it banishes blemishes too.

Several compounds in bergamot oil have antibacterial and anti-inflammatory properties. This may make bergamot oil an effective spot treatment for acne in people who do not have sensitive skin. Its analgesic qualities may also make it effective against painful cysts and pimples.

KOREAN INSPIRED RICE CREAM

This cream has anti-aging and brightening effects and it can be applied to all types of skin. This Rice Cream is Korean inspired and it will make your skin fair, glowing, radiant, and spotless within few days and will also help in removing all your acne, blemishes, dark spots, and pigmentation rapidly.

INGREDIENTS

White Rice	3 tbs
Aloe Vera Gel (ready-made in the market or freshly taken from peeled leaf)	1 tbs
Glycerin	1 ts
Vitamin E	1/2 ts
Pure Frankincense (for oily skin) or Rosehip (for dry or normal skin) Essential oil	8 drops
Water	2-3 glass

DIRECTION

1. Wash the rice properly.
2. Add rice and water into the pan and let it cook until it becomes mushy and thick.
3. Strain the overcooked rice with the help of a strainer to take out all the rice paste.
4. Now add all the other ingredients to the paste and stir it well to get the creamy and thick paste.
5. (You may use the food processor to get the softer creamy paste.)
6. Your cream is ready, transfer it to the small airtight container.
7. You may keep your cream in the fridge for up to 15 days.

--- *Benefit* ---

White rice is rich in vitamin B and it is a powerful antioxidant that boosts collagen production and removes wrinkles and fine lines White rice has been used as a natural beauty ingredient for 1000 of years in Korea, China, and Japan.

Vitamin E helps support the immune system, cell function, and skin health. It's an antioxidant, making it effective at combating the effects of free radicals produced by the metabolism of food and toxins in the environment. Vitamin E may be beneficial at reducing UV damage to the skin.

Glycerin is a humectant, a type of moisturizing agent that pulls water into the outer layer of your skin from deeper levels of your skin and the air.

MYEONYAK FACIAL MEDICINE

Eggs can be used in improving skin texture. Egg yolks are rich in fatty acids that can lend moisture to the skin while the egg whites contain albumin, a simple form of protein that helps tighten pores and also remove excessive oil.

INGREDIENTS

Eggs 3

White wine

Rosehip Essential Oil 10 drops

Glass Jar with tide lid

DIRECTION

1. Place three eggs and wine into the jar and seal it airtight. Let your Magical Mix stand for about one month. After one month, add 10 drops of Rose essential oil to your creamy fusion and apply it on your face. It will not only relieve the chapped skin but also make your skin glow like jade.

CHAPTER 06

MYSTERIOUS EGYPT

Queen Nefertari Beauty Secrets/ 71
Queen Cleopatra's Beauty Recipes/ 74
Cleopatra's Bath/ 74
Cleopatra's Cream/ 75

CHAPTER 06

MYSTERIOUS EGYPT

MYSTERIOUS EGYPT

I didn't want to stop finding out more about skincare rituals from ancient times. I took different books, research papers, and other resources from which I could extract the Greek and Egyptian recipes responsible for their exotic beauty.

No other culture has been so influenced by the concept of beautification and body care as Egyptians. Egyptian queens like Nefertiti had their own blend of kohl which was found to have antibacterial properties. But even the lowliest of citizens were supplied olive oil with their wages so that they could care for their bodies.

Greeks and Ancient Egyptians had baths also known as aromatic or medicinal bath as their prominent feature. They considered it to be a holistic therapy for protection infections, anti-aging, longevity, shine, and beauty. Essential oils, fragrant plants, and various herbs containing soaps were infused in water to treat and relax bodies and rejuvenate skin. Herbal bath's fame has still not subsided. In many parts of the world, it is being used as a spiritual therapy and for the enhancement and sprucing up of the skin.

It is known that the Queen of Egypt, Cleopatra, bathed with rose petals and milk for hours and exfoliate her body with Dead Sea salt. It is a famous ritual that is inherited predecessors and is being cherished till today. Bathing therapy leaves your body and mind relaxed while your skin enjoys the pampering.

A mixture of clay and crushed beetles used as a cheek blush. Only women from high society were allowed to have long hair and slave women had to cut their hair very short which were often used for making headpieces for the aristocrats. Ancient Egyptians made eyeliners from lead-based kohl.

Ancient Egyptians made soap using clay and olive oil, which would not only cleanse but also nourish and heal the skin.

Wealthy Egyptian women have carried out the most refined beauty ritual at their toilets before bed. They could be used to apply incense pellets to their underarms as deodorant, and floral or spice-infused oils to soften their skin.

From the earliest era of the Egyptian empire (around 6000 B.C.E.), men and women from all social classes liberally applied eyeliner, eyeshadow, lipstick, and rouge by mixing the powdered malachite, black kohl, and crushed beetles with animal fat or vegetable oils.

Egyptians also invented a natural method of waxing with a mixture of honey and sugar.

In death, too, the personal appearance was so serious to Egyptian identity. Burial sites uncovered from the very beginning of the society's history, in Predynastic times, show that it was common for Egyptians to include everyday items like combs, scented ointments, jewelry, and cosmetics (many examples found with makeup still inside them) in the graves of men, women, and children.

Every civilization has ingredients which are famous in their skincare regime. Sandalwood, honey, and oatmeal were widely used in Egyptian skincare regimes. The benefits of these have been celebrated since ages.

The properties of sandalwood powder soothes skin in the hot weather and to even the skin tone. Sandal powder has a woody intense scent and is revered for the healing properties that it carries. Its use can be found in Ayurveda as well. These Ayurvedic medicines have not only been beneficial for skin but various other health issues as well. Since it is an antiseptic and inflammatory agent it can heal, protect, and improve your way drastically and significantly. To make one attractive for others sandal is converted into scents which is classic and alluring. Sandal has been preferred as a scent by high-end brands and is listed among the best scents. It is used to address problems like common cold, urinary tract infections, liver, gallbladder, digestive, and muscle. Furthermore, serious illnesses like mental disorders, hemorrhoids, and scabies. During the days when you feel low and anxious sandalwood is your go-to product for calming yourself down. It was applied in a paste form to heal wounds as the olfactory receptors of skin react actively to it. Moreover, common skin issues like acne, dark circles, dark spots and suntan which occur due to hectic lifestyles and exposure to environmental pollutants can be curbed with sandalwood. It has proved itself to be a curing herb and this gives it an edge over many other chemical products available in the market.

Another such product is honey, which has been acknowledged by Ayurveda and organic skin care experts. It is a famous wound healer. The properties that it contains have allowed it to be a part of the world of medicine for over 5,000 years. It does not only treat wounds orally, but it also treats your body from the inside. It is preferred to include it in your daily diet as it gives you various nutrients essential for your hormones and body. Honey is rich in phenolic compounds like flavonoids and organic acids, which are some of the sources to strengthen your immune system and increase the antioxidant value of blood. It is an agent to delay and eliminate the risk of heart disease and people affected by type 2 diabetes. The antioxidants compound lower the blood pressure considerably. Honey improves the cholesterol level of patients suffering from high LDL cholesterol levels. The topical honey treatment has been used to heal wounds and burns since ancient Egyptand is practiced today.

The antibacterial and anti-inflammatory properties enable the nourishment of the surrounding tissues when applied to cater to the wounds resulting in their recovery. Its treatments allow medicine practitioners to impact psoriasis and herpes lesions significantly. Furthermore, diabetic foot ulcers can be cured at times from the application of honey or medicines having honey as their components. Antiseptic and antibacterial qualities of honey help in the cure of acne and dryness. It keeps the skin hydrated and moisturised. It is widely used in cosmetics to healing scars and evening out skin tone. Eczema, psoriasis, and inflam- mation are subsided with the application of honey.

Oatmeal is one of the most fruitful breakfasts for people looking for meals to benefit their skin and heart. It comes with a plethora of prospects that can affect a person in a great manner. One of the key benefits of oatmeal for skin is its amazing ability to anti-aging. It has reparative properties for skins of all kinds, including sensitive and damaged skins. It produces a healthy and protective layer that helps enormously in retaining the natural moisture of the skin. Furthermore, it aids a lot in reducing skin inflammation that is one of the biggest advantages of oatmeal when it comes to protecting the skin. It stimulates collagen production due to the rich beta-glucan available in it. Moreover, it keeps the skin hydrated by making a defensive fence that can take water to the skin.

The Egyptian practices can be adopted successfully to improve your overall health of skin. These are responsible for keeping your skin youthful and glowing. I personally believe that it is essential to have one or more of these recipes included in your daily routine.

Along with your skin, oatmeal aids in weight loss. It is a meal that is full of nutrients, carbs, and fibers. It is a grain which is relatively higher than the other grains. A bowl of these suffice for an entire meal and its intake aids in keeping the body fit and loss of excessive weight.

QUEEN NEFERTARI BEAUTY SECRETS

QUEEN NEFERTARI BEAUTY SECRETS (SANDALWOOD FACE MASK)

This face mask recipe using sandalwood oil claimed that was used by Queen Nefertari to reduce wrinkles and sun damage, and helped her look young until the age of 100.

INGREDIENTS		DIRECTION
Plain Full-fat Greek Yoghurt	1 tbs	1. Mix the ingredients and Cover your face, neck.
Raw Honey	1 ts	2. Leave it for 30 minutes and wash it with water.
pure sandalwood essential oil	8 drops	3. You may apply this mask twice a week before bed.

MIX

APPLY TO FACE

WASH AFTER 30 MIN

HONEY FACIAL SCRUB

INGREDIENTS		DIRECTION
Honey	1 tbs	You need to apply this scrub immediately after mixing and massage your skin for 5 minutes and rinse well.
Natron or Baking Soda	1 tap	
Myrrh Essential Oil	2 drops	

MIX

APPLY TO SKIN

RINSE AFTER 5 MIN

HAIR GROWTH STIMULATOR

INGREDIENTS

Castor Oil	4 tbs
Almond Oil	4 tbs
Olive Oil	2 tbs
Rosemary Essential Oil	10 drops

FOLLOW DIRECTION   APPLY TO HAIR AND COVER   WASH AFTER SEVEAL HOURS

DIRECTION

1. Mix all oils together in a bowl and heat it before using it.
2. Place this bowl in a pan half-filled with water and heat the pan till water boil.
3. Leave it for 5 minutes and remove the bowl.
4. Pour your hot mix into the spray bottle and spray it into your scalp and hair.
5. If you don't have a spray bottle, you may apply the oil on your scalp with a piece of cotton.
6. Cover your head with a towel and leave it for an hour.
7. You can even leave it on overnight, washing it the next morning.
8. This will give the oil ample time to do its work.

Benefit

Castor oil is derived from castor bean that contains antioxidants, vitamin E, and proteins which help in voluminous and lustrous hair growth. Invest in cold-pressed castor oil as it is more beneficial in controlling hair loss and preventing split ends.

Rosemary oil stimulates blood flow to the scalp. It helps preserve the hair colour, delaying the onset of grey hair. Moreover, it is known to increase hair thickness at the same rate as minoxidil does. Regular application of diluted rosemary oil can help combat patchy hair loss and propel the regrowth of natural hair.

QUEEN'S TREASURE OIL

From burial sites and hieroglyphics, archaeologists have determined that ancient Egyptians used a variety of plant-based oils on their hair and skin, and this special mix was one of their treasured scents and the most adored one that would find in royal women's makeup box.

INGREDIENTS

Argan Oil — 50 ml

Myrrh Essential Oil — 10 drops

Frankincense Essential Oil — 12 drops

FOLLOW DIRECTION

APPLY TO HAIR AND COVER

WASH AFTER SEVEAL HOURS

DIRECTION

1. Mix all these ingredients with an incredible smell in a small glass dropper bottle or pump bottle.
2. You may use it as a natural anti-aging and skin smoothing serum or face oil on your face every night after cleaning your face.
3. Or you can use it as hair oil and apply it on your scalp down till the entire length of your hair to get manageable and shiny hair and get rid of dandruff or itchy scalp and stimulate your hair growth

Benefit

Argan oil is mostly used as a moisturizer for skin and hair because it is full of fatty acids, mainly oleic acid and linoleic acid. Argan oil is also rich in vitamin E, which provides a fatty layer to your hair and scalp that may help prevent dryness and can help reduce fizziness and boost

Myrrh Essential Oil's astringency strengthens the roots and thus reduces hair loss. Along with addressing dandruff, its scent also stimulates the brain, promotes alertness, and boosts energy. Packed with antioxidants, myrrh is great for anti-aging, skin rejuvenation, or healing of wounds. It encourages new cell growth and reduces wrinkles.

Frankincense essential oil is said to treat dry skin and reduce the appearance of wrinkles, age spots, scars, and stretch marks. Frankincense essential oil is also used to help slow (and ultimately prevent) hair loss, as well as stimulate hair growth when applied topically to the scalp. Frankincense contains Vitamin E which helps to nourish and strengthen the hair from within.

QUEEN CLEOPATRA'S BEAUTY RECIPES

AMAZING FACE CREAM FOR GLOWING SKIN

INGREDIENTS

Aloe vera Gel	2 tbs
Myrrh Essential Oil	4 drops
Almond Oil	1 tbs
Beewax	2 ts
Vitamin E Capsule	1

DIRECTION

1. Heat the beeswax and the almond oil until the substance gets liquid, then add the rest of the ingredients
2. After the cream cools down, you can put it into your fridge
3. Apply it as a night cream after cleaning your face and before sleep. It can last for about a week.

FOLLOW DIRECTON

APPLY TO FACE AS NIGHT CREAM

CLEOPATRA'S BATH

For baths, Cleopatra used to mix milk of a young donkey with fresh honey, almond oil, and her holistic essential oils. This was her secret for soft and glowing skin.

INGREDIENTS

Honey	1/2 cup
Fresh full-fat milk (or 2 cups of milk powder)	4 cup
Almond oil or olive oil	5 tbs
Each Myrrh, Rose and Essential oil or Frankincense Essential Oil	15 drops

DIRECTION

To prepare this gorgeous milk and honey bath. Mix all ingredients, then pour this substance into your bath and make your skin gentle and silky!

CLEOPATRA'S CREAM

INGREDIENTS

dry weight Tallow Balm (1 cup when melted down)	200 gr
Sweet Almond oil	1/4 cup
Each Myrrh, Rose and Frankincense Essential Oil	15 drops

FOLLOW DIRECTON

APPLY TO FACE AS CREAM

DIRECTION

1. In a double boiler, melt the tallow.
2. In a medium mixing bowl, combine melted tallow and the almond oil.
3. Place the bowl in the fridge to let it harden.
4. Using a hand mixer, whip until very fluffy. Scrape the sides as you go. This is key to getting a nice texture to spread it on your face, so do not skimp on this step. You want it to look like whipped frosting.
5. While whipping, add in the essential oils.
6. Spoon it into small glass jars.
7. Makes about 2 jars full. Store the second jar in the fridge to keep it fresher longer.
8. Smooth your balm on your face 1-2 times a day and watch your skin's transformation!

---
benefit

Tallow contains the abundant fat-soluble activators — vitamins A, D, E, and K — which are necessary for skin health. It also contains conjugated linoleic acid (CLA) which has anti-inflammatory properties.

CLEOPATRA'S GRAPE FACIAL

INGREDIENTS

Honey	1 tbs
Green Grape	1/2 cup

MIX — APPLY TO SKIN & MASSAGE — RINSE AFTER 15 MIN

DIRECTION

1. Crush green grapes to a pulp and add honey to it and mix together.
2. Apply on a clean face and leave it for 15 minutes.
3. After 15 minutes massage it into your skin and rinse off with warm water.

CLEOPATRA'S NATURAL BEAUTY SOAP

Another beauty secret of Cleopatra is that she loved using oatmeal to cleanse her skin. Oatmeal not only cleanses the skin it also eliminates the dirt and exfoliates the dead skin. It mosturises and nourishes the skin. Soaps can be a bit harsh on the skin so try using this natural soap for beautiful skin.

INGREDIENTS

Oatmeal	1 tbs
Rose Water	-
Coconut oil	1/2 ts

DIRECTION

1. To cleanse the skin using oatmeal mix oats with warm Rosewater in a bowl and wait until the oats get soft.
2. Add coconut oil and then gently massage the soft oats away all over your face and body for about 3-4 minutes.
3. Rinse off your skin with warm and then cold water to moisturise the skin.

CHAPTER 07

GRAND PERSIA

Sidr & Yogurt Hair Mask / 82
How To Make Sormeh / 83
Saffron & Sandalwood Face Mask / 84
Saffron Face Pack For Dull Skin / 85
Potato Starch Masks to lighten the skin colour / 87
Pomegranate & Papaya Face Pack For Glowing Skin / 88

CHAPTER 06
GRAND PERSIA

THE ANCIENT PERSIAN NATURAL BEAUTY SECRETS

Persian beauty and Gorgeous looking girls with shiny volumed hair and soft glowing skin have been adored for centuries. But behind that loveliness, Persian just use some natural ingredients in treating their body to be wonderful. Grandmothers and mothers would pass down certain rituals to their daughters for centuries; therefore the lineage of these ancient methods are still alive today.

I remember my mother and aunts sharing their beauty secrets and relationship advice as they painted their nails, beat white eggs mixed with honey and yogurt for a smooth facial mask or applied a olive oil, chamomile and egg yolk mask to enhance blonde highlights in their hair. The taste of mashed tomato as it dripped from my cheeks and the stickiness of honey on my lips is how I remember those long summer evenings.

Weekly exfoliating and scrubbing rituals With Kiseh and Sefidab were mandatory to remove dead skin, release toxins and allow for new energy. Sefitab, which is an exfoliating chunk of hardened minerals and sheep fat. Sefitab, which means "white water" looks like a small chalk ball; however, it's an ancient formula made specifically for removing dead skin and polishing the skin until it's as soft as velvet.

Oil is essentially used daily to smooth and nourishes hair and skin. They use different kind of oil such as olive, sesame, almond, and coconut oil. Daily application before bed time and leave it over-night, will prevent skin from dryness. These oils are Persian's must-have item as it gives many bene-fits for daily body care. Oil has also been one of the basic ingredients for a mixture. Combining drops of almond oil with honey, works wonders to treat dry and chopped lips.

Persian queen are acquainted to bathing in keeping their skin satin-smooth. Their routines vary from milk bath, oil bath, to Dead Sea salt bath to combat stress, aging, and improve blood circula-tion.

Rose water and Honey are two most common ingredients that all Persian women must have in their house since 2000 years ago. Both Rose water and honey are nature's best moisturizer thus it will well-hydrated the face. However, it is best to use high quality pure ones to give maximum ben-efit and soothe minor face problem such as acne, blemishes, and scars.

Sidr

The other Iranian beauty secrets for hair and skin is sedr, which comes from the leaves of the lotus tree. The Sidr, also known as Jujube, allows you to do hair care and brings a lot of benefits: rich in saponins, this vegetable ingredient was the main hair wash product when shampoo was not invented. ... Sidr powder can also be beneficial for skin problems such as acne, psoriasis, eczema ... Moreover, it soothes the itching. Almost most of Iranian women know that the sidr how to tackle dandruff , strengthens and conditions hair, and giving it a glossy shine with the mixture of sidr powder and water.

SIDR & YOGURT HAIR MASK

Sidr Powder works on all types of hair, but is especially recommended for treating dandruff hair, colored hair and sensitive scalp hair. To reduce the itchy scalp and irritation, Sidr powder is perfect. Washing the hair with this powder then leave a mask on wet hair helps promote hair growth too.

INGREDIENTS

- Sidr Powder — 4 tbs
- Yogurt — 5 tbs
- Olive Oil — 2 tbs
- Warm Water

DIRECTION

1. Mix Sidr powder with yogurt and olive oil and a little warm water, then leave the mixture for 30 minutes to ferment.
2. Apply this mask to your hair to the end, leave it for three hours then rinse off your hair.

MIX — APPLY TO HAIR — RINSE AFTER 3 HOURS

--- S I D R ---

Sidr and henna mask to remove skin blemishes

To get rid of pimples and remove blemishes and dullness of your skin, mix some colorless henna and side powder in equal amounts and apply it on your skin twice a week to see how the dullness of the skin fades over time and clear and glowing skin will show up.

Sidr mask and case for hair loss

Combine 50 grams of colorless henna with 150 grams of cedar and 150 grams of case and put it on the hair, wash your hair after half an hour, this mask is great for preventing hair loss and strengthens the hair roots.

Sidr and lemon juice mask to whiten hands

To whiten your hands and body, combine Sidr Powder and lemon juice to make a paste that is nei-ther firm nor too loose, then apply it to all parts of your body and wash off 15 minutes later.

Sidr and bitter almond oil to brighter and clear skin

To make the mask, Mix one tablespoon of side powder with one glass of water and let it boil for 5 minutes. mix the juice with the same amount of bitter almond oil, now put it on low heat, stir gently until the juice evaporates and the cedar extract remains in the almond oil. Let it cool down and apply it on your face and neck for 20 to 40 minutes. The longer this mask stays on the skin, the more effective it will be. It will give you a brighter and clear skin.

White teeth

Other secret weapon for white teeth was passed down to us from our grandmothers is from Neyshabur, the northeastern city most famous for poets Khayyam and Attar and, as it so hap-pens, rhubarb (Rivas). Rhubarb powder is not only a natural whitener, but it's also good for other dental problems and the gums. You just dip a wet toothbrush in some powder and brush your teeth normally.

SORMEH

Sormeh is a natural eyeliner that many Middle Eastern women use, and Iranian women are no ex-ception. It's made from various nuts like almonds, walnuts, pistachios, and hazelnuts which are roasted until black and then ground into soot.

How to make sormeh

Just Use one almond or hazelnut . Burn it till halfway covered with black soot. Scrape soot into the bowling avoid any almond chunks. Add few drops of almond oil to get the smooth paste. Your eyeliner is ready. keep this paste in a small container.

SAFFRON

Last but not the least, Saffron, Red God, was initially widely cultivated in Iran, India, and Greece and apart from using it as a delicate flavoring in exotic dishes , It was also used in herbal medicine in these countries. It has antimutagenic, antihypertensive, antitussive, cytotoxic, anticonvulsant, and many other beneficial effects on the body when ingested. Saffron is also known to improve memory and learning skills. Its benefits for the skin were also realized and natural medicine specialists start-ed adding it to face packs and topical creams.

How to use saffron

- Take the saffron threads you intend to use for the recipe and crush them into a powder using a mortar and pestle. If you don't have a mortar and pestle, you can crumble the threads in between your fingers.
- Steep the crushed saffron in warm water, stock, milk, or white wine and keep it in a warm place for 20 to 30 minutes. If there's any liquid in your recipe, use a small amount of the specified liq-uid from the instructions.
- Add the saffron and soaking liquids directly to your recipe when called for.

SAFFRON & SANDALWOOD FACE MASK

Apply this homemade saffron facial mask at least once a week for a radiant and smooth skin. You can use this pack up to 3 times a week. Sandalwood enhances the complexion and makes your skin smooth and radiant.

INGREDIENTS		DIRECTION
Sandalwood Powder	1 tbs	1. Mix all the ingredients together.
Saffron Strands	3 - 4	2. Apply the paste on your freshly washed face. Spread the pack evenly all over your face.
Milk or Rosewater (if you are sensitive to dairy products)	2 ts	3. Massage while still damp in a circular motion and then, let it dry for 20 minutes.
		4. Rinse it off by splashing water over your

MIX

APPLY TO FACE

RINSE AFTER 20 MIN

SAFFRON & SUNFLOWER SEEDS FACE PACK

Use this face pack twice a week. This face mask makes your skin fair and rosy. Sunflower seed contains oils that act as emollients when applied topically. It is rich in vitamin E.

INGREDIENTS		DIRECTION
Sunflower Seeds	3 - 4	1. Soak the sunflower seeds and saffron in warm milk or rosewater overnight.
Saffron Strands	3 - 4	2. In the morning, grind this mixture and apply the resultant paste on your skin.
Milk or Rosewater (if you are sensitive to dairy products)	1/4 cup	3. Keep this on until it dries and then rinse your face.

MIX

APPLY TO FACE

RINSE AFTER 20 MIN

SAFFRON FACE PACK FOR DULL SKIN

Use this face pack twice a week. This face pack reduces dullness of the face and freshens it up. Bengal gram absorbs all the dirt, grime, and grease. It also exfoliates the skin.

INGREDIENTS

saffron strands	7 - 8
Milk	2 tbs
Bengal Gram	1 tbs

DIRECTION

1. Soak the Bengal gram in milk overnight.
2. Grind the soaked gram along with the same milk and the saffron strands.
3. Apply this pack on the face.
4. Wash it off after 15-20 minutes, once it has dried.

FOLLOW DIRECTION

APPLY TO FACE

WASH AFTER 15-20 MIN

SAFFRON & OLIVE OIL FOR GLOWING SKIN

Coconut oil, almond oil, or sesame oil can also be used instead of olive oil. Repeat this every alternate night. The massage with the saffron-infused oil will improve circulation to the skin and give it a beautiful glow. Massaging will also help the nourishing fatty acids from the oil to get absorbed easily into the skin

INGREDIENTS

Saffron Strands	3 - 4
Olive Oil	1 tbs

DIRECTION

1. Thoroughly mix the saffron strands in the warm oil.
2. Massage the skin in upward motions using this oil.
3. Wipe the oil off after an hour using a wet tissue.
4. You can leave this oil on overnight as well.

MIX

APPLY WITH MASSAGE

WIPE OFF AFTER 1 HOUR

SAFFRON AND HONEY FACE PACK

The antioxidants present in honey can help you to get rid of blemishes, dark spots, and scars from your skin. Honey also helps to lock the moisture into the skin.

INGREDIENTS		DIRECTION
Honey	1 tbs	1. Mix honey with the saffron strands.
Saffron Strands	2 - 3	2. Massage the facial skin with this using upward circular motions.

MIX   APPLY TO FACE   RINSE AFTER 8-10 MIN

3. Leave the saffron-honey mixture on the skin for 8-10 minutes before rinsing it off with water.
4. Apply this once in every 2-3 days.

POTATO

Since Persian women have always desired to have a bright and spot free skin, Potato starch and potato were the other favourable ingredients in their DIY home care. I have totally uncovered six ways that this underground dwelling friend can help your skin and hair look awesome!

1. By using cold potato juice as a daily facial rinse, you can say goodbye to unwanted dark spots. Grate your potato and refrigerate the juice to keep it cool and fresh.

2. Potatoes are great for treating sunburned skin and can even help relieve the pain. Cut a cold potato into thin slices and place them over the affected areas to soothe and cool skin.

3. The humble potato can act as a natural skin brightener to help diminish the appearance of dark circles under eyes. Peel and slice a raw potato into large pieces (enough to cover the eye area) then get two pieces of cloth and wrap a piece of potato into each. Place the cloths over your eyes for 15 to 20 minutes before washing off with warm water. Repeat regularly and watch the magic happen.

4. Potato can help to banish wrinkles and act as an anti aging treatment. Dip a cotton ball or soft cloth into potato juice and dab your face gently to keep your skin soft and glowing.

5. Potatoes can also be used to remove dead skin cells from the face. Apply grated, peeled potato to the skin for 10 minutes and rinse with warm water. Doing so regularly will keep your skin feel-ing fresh and soft as a baby's bottom.

6. Potato will reduce the Appearance of Scars. A simple potato and lemon mix can go a long way! Blend potato and lemon juice and apply to any facial scars or marks. Leave the mixture on the ar-ea for 20 minutes before rinsing with warm water.

POTATO STARCH MASKS TO LIGHTEN THE SKIN COLOR

INGREDIENTS		DIRECTION
Yogurt	2 tbs	Mix all the ingredients till you get the homogenous mixture and apply it on your skin for 20 minutes and rinse off with warm water. Repeat this recipe twice a week to get favourable result.
Potato Starch	1 tbs	
Lemon Juice	1 ts	
OR		
Rose Water	2 tbs	
Potato Starch	1 tbs	
Honey	1 tbs	

MIX

APPLY TO SKIN

WASH AFTER 20 MIN

POMEGRANATE

The pomegranate, one of the world's most ancient fruits, has had a long and fascinating history. Although it probably originated in Persia, cultivation spread quickly throughout the Mediterranean and extended to Arabia, Afghanistan, India and China, where it was called the "Chinese apple," the alternate appellation.

Before I move on to how you can incorporate pomegranate in your beauty regimen, let's check out some of its beauty benefits.

1. Keep Your Skin Hydrated

The juice of pomegranate replenishes the moisture levels of your skin and keeps it hydrated. It is an excellent source of vitamin C, which makes your skin soft and smooth by reducing dryness. When applied topically, the oil contained in pomegranate seeds promotes regeneration of the epidermis (outer layer of skin) and skin repair.

2. Protect Your Skin From Environmental And Sun Damage

Exposure to the harmful UV rays damages your skin, but pomegranate can prevent this. It contains anthocyanin, tannins, and antioxidants that have anti-inflammatory properties and reduce UVB damage.

3. Have Anti-Aging Benefits

A study indicated that pomegranate extracts could reduce the effects of photoaging while increas-ing collagen type I, hyaluronan, and water content of the skin. They also have an anti-oxidative im-pact on the skin.

Here's how you can use pomegranate to get glowing skin

POMEGRANATE SEED AND LEMON JUICE FOR SUNTAN TREATING

Honey moisturizes your skin, and pomegranate keeps it hydrated, making it baby soft.

INGREDIENTS		DIRECTION

Pomegranate Paste (blend a few seeds to get the paste)	1 tbs	1. Mix all ingredients to get a soft paste. 2. Apply the paste to your face and neck (and any other exposed and tanned areas). 3. Keep it on for at least 30 minutes and then wash it off. 4. You may try this recipe Twice or thrice a
Lemon Juice	1/2 ts	
Honey	1 ts	

MIX

APPLY TO FACE AND NECK

WASH AFTER 30 MIN

POMEGRANATE & PAPAYA FACE PACK FOR GLOWING SKIN

A face mask blend of pomegranate and cocoa powder will help you achieve youthful skin in no time. This mix is loaded with anti-ageing properties and antioxidants that will help you get that glow

INGREDIENTS	
Pomegranate Paste	1 tbs
Cocoa Powder	1 tbs

DIRECTION

1. Mix pomegranate paste with cocoa powder.
2. Add water if the consistency is too thick.
3. Apply the mask to your face and let it dry.
4. Wash it off with cold water.

MIX

APPLY TO FACE

POMEGRANATE AND OATMEAL FACE MASK FOR REVITALISING YOUR SKIN

Honey is also super moisturising for your skin. Oatmeal acts as an exfoliator. When you combine it with pomegranate transform dull and damaged skin into soft and clear skin.

INGREDIENTS		DIRECTION
Pomegranate Seed	1/2 cup	1. Grind the pomegranate seeds and make a paste.
Oatmeal	2 tbs	2. Mix the oatmeal powder and honey with the paste and blend well.
Honey	1 tbs	3. Apply this mask to your face and massage with gentle circular strokes.

FOLLOW DIRECTION   APPLY TO FACE AND MASSAGE   WASH AFTER 30 MIN

4. Leave it on for about 30 minutes and then wash with cold water.
5. You may apply this mask once a week.

POMEGRANATE, ALMOND OIL, AND RICE

This face pack tones your face and reduces the signs of aging and is extremely beneficial for those with combination skin. Almond oil keeps the skin moisturized and hydrated.

INGREDIENTS		DIRECTION
Pomegranate Seed (make a paste)	1/2 cup	1. In a bowl, put all the ingredients and mix them well until they form a thick consistent paste.
Rice Flour	1 tbs	2. Apply this mixture to your face and neck and let it sit for a good 15-20 minutes before rinsing it off.
Almond Oil	3-4 drops	

MIX   APPLY TO FACE AND NECK   WASH AFTER 15 - 20 MIN

POMEGRANATE PEEL, BESAN, AND MILK CREAM

If you have super dry skin, try this face mask. Milk is known for its moisturizing and skin lightening benefits while besan exfoliates the skin and unclogs the pores. (leave pomegranate peels in the sun to dry and then make powder)

INGREDIENTS	
Pomegranate Peel Powder	2 tbs
Besan	1 tbs
milk cream	2 tbs

DIRECTION

1. Mix all the ingredients well to make a smooth paste
2. apply this paste to your face and neck.
3. Leave it on for about 20 minutes and then wash it off.
4. You can use this mask twice a week.

 MIX  APPLY TO FACE AND NECK   RINSE AFTER 20 MIN

POMEGRANATE PEEL, ROSEWATER, AND LEMON

Lemon is an excellent exfoliator and skin brightening agent. This face pack brightens your skin tone. You will notice the difference right from the first usage.

INGREDIENTS	
Pomegranate Peel Powder	3 tbs
Lemon Juice	1 tbs
Rose Water	2 ts

DIRECTION

1. Mix all the ingredients in a bowl and make sure that the paste is not too thick.
2. Once done, apply this paste to your face and neck and leave it on for a good 20 minutes.
3. Wash it with cold water after-wards.

 MIX  APPLY TO FACE AND NECK  RINSE AFTER 20 MIN

My exploration and gave me an insight that along with Essential oil, there are any other organic products that we include in our beauty regime and get the desired glowing skin, which we all dream about. Skin rituals are being carried out for decades and transferred from generation to generation, which can have positive impacts on our skin naturally when incorporated into our daily routine. Natural products show their results when used steadily; however, they do not harm your skin, like chemical products used in cosmetics and other formulas related to skin.

The skin is a part of your immune system as it acts as a barrier between your inner parts of the body and external forces. Infections, bacteria, and pathogens, and viruses are held back by different layers of our skin. Moreover, the skin is responsible for various important activities of the body. These activities include temperature regulation, insulation, sensation, synthesis of vitamin D. It is one of the most important parts of your body. It not only indicates your beauty, but it is a protective layer that requires nourishment and moisture. With different ways and recipes, you can add beneficial rituals to your routine, benefiting the skin. Your hair and skin define your beauty, and appear beautiful are what each one of us desires. But, a better approach is to keep it healthy and strengthened along with maintaining its beauty. The quality of your skin improves when a proper skin routine is followed. As the most eye-catching part of our appearance, it shouldn't be neglected. Your skin gives an overall idea of your health. It is affected when your body is not in proper shape or is facing ailments. It is often noted that skincare is not taken as seriously by people as it should. People skip investing time and money on skincare products as it is a perception that it does not significantly affect the skin. However, there should be awareness of the essentiality of the skin care regime. People who use skincare products as rituals feel a drastic change in their skin's condition and health. To think that looking after your skin is expensive and tiresome does not work in your favor. You need to think beyond the current times and look after your skin and hair for the sake of staying beautiful and maintaining health. Once you set a routine of your skincare regime, you would see a notable difference in your skin and hair. Beauty can fade away; however, with proper care, you can delay the process. The epidermis of your skin requires replenishing, revitalization, and regeneration, which is only possible with the amalgamation of the right products.

When different products come together, they release their nutrients, minerals, and vitamins, which get absorbed in your skin. The complimenting of these compounds makes your skin glowing, elastic, and refined. The skin is of various types, and therefore, you can try different products to choose the most appropriate one for your skin. There is no fear of trying these recipes as they are organic and don't harm the skin.

I have adapted these and I want to wholeheartedly extend the recipes and information to all those who love their skin and would grab every opportunity to keep it healthy with Essential Oils, organic and natural products.

www.ingramcontent.com/pod-product-compliance
Lightning Source LLC
Chambersburg PA
CBHW040416100526
44588CB00022B/2850